D1650581

One Man's War

I2232352

One Man's War

An Essex Soldier
in World War Two

Ron Davies

Edited by Bill Davies

TEMPUS

SANDWELL LIBRARY &
INFORMATION SERVICE

12232352	
Bertrams	13/01/2009
940.548141	£9.99
HA	

Frontispiece: .... 1944, 451 Battery Essex
Yeomanry. Courtesy of Mrs L. Davies.

First published 2008

Tempus Publishing
The History Press Ltd.
Cirencester Road, Chalford
Stroud, Gloucestershire, GL6 8PE
www.thehistorypress.co.uk

Tempus Publishing is an imprint of The History Press Ltd.

© Bill Davies, 2008

The right of Bill Davies to be identified as the Author
of this work has been asserted in accordance with the
Copyrights, Designs and Patents Act 1988.

All rights reserved. No part of this book may be reprinted
or reproduced or utilised in any form or by any electronic,
mechanical or other means, now known or hereafter invented,
including photocopying and recording, or in any information
storage or retrieval system, without the permission in writing
from the Publishers.

British Library Cataloguing in Publication Data.
A catalogue record for this book is available from the British Library.

ISBN 978 0 7524 4517 5

Typesetting and origination by The History Press Ltd.
Printed in Great Britain

Contents

Father and Son

I happened to glance in the mirror today
And there, looking back at me, was my father.
He didn't say anything, just stared intently,
Seemingly curious, with a sad little smile.

There were the same brown-flecked sleepy green eyes,
The same nose, chin, and cupid's bow mouth
But the curly mop on top could not be his,
And I came back to reality with a gentle bump

We stared at each other, father and son,
And within the space of a nano-second
I saw his life, his essence, the complete man,
The soldier, the entertainer, the family anchor

In my mind I smiled back and said 'Hi Dad,
I always knew you hadn't gone away
You were here all the time, just hiding,
I only had to look for you within myself'.

FBSR Bill Davies 23 April 2004

Ron and Lily with baby Bill. Courtesy of Mrs L. Davies.

Preface

This is essentially a personal account of the experiences and memories of an ordinary soldier during the Second World War. Ron 'Popeye' Davies joined the Territorial Army before the war started, but he did not see action until 6 June 1944, D-Day. The preceding four years seemed to be just one long rehearsal for the invasion, but they were far from dull – his training years were full of drama, incident, and humour, and throughout the narrative Ron reveals his emotions and thoughts. His unique writing style allows the reader to see the war through his eyes, and he lets us into his life and those of his comrades.

He gives a brief account of his childhood during the Depression, a testament to the ability and courage of his parents. He draws fantastic word pictures of the characters who shaped his life: his formidable mother, his musician father, and his Aunt Carrie who ran a seafront café in Liverpool.

When war was declared Ron was called up, and became a tank gunner or 'Bombardier' with the Essex Yeomanry. After describing the build-up to D-Day he takes us through the invasion minute by minute, with the continuous action laid out in graphic detail. The Allied push through France, Belgium, and Holland, as seen through Ron's eyes, is dangerous and exhausting, but the regiment had a well-deserved rest at Heerlen, where Ron met the hospitable Plönes family.

The regiment crossed the Rhine into Germany, and after a heartbreaking round of duty at Belsen they pushed on to the Baltic coast. VE day came and went, but Ron was still engaged in 'mopping up' groups of SS fanatics who fought to the death. He stayed at Kiel for eighteen months after the war, guarding high-profile Nazi prisoners, and, before he accepted his 'Demob', he qualified as a Regimental PTI.

Left: Dad's blazer badge. Courtesy of Mrs L. Davies.

Below: Ron's medals: The Defence Medal, Service Medal, 1939–1945 Star, France and Germany Star, Campaign Medal. Courtesy of Mrs L. Davies.

Foreword

How difficult it must be to write a book using rough notes left by your father, and using all the stories that he had told you about his life and his experiences during the war.

It is a wonderful story written so well by Popeye's son, Bill. It is inevitable that in one or two places the lines get a little crossed and there are some minor historical inaccuracies, but Popeye was a remarkable young man and his stories about the events are marvellous. He was also a great entertainer.

The Essex Yeomanry were a very special team of comrades that managed to compete so well with all the tasks that were set for them, and we still meet together from time to time.

The friendships that were established in those days over sixty years ago still remain, and if we can remember what happened yesterday we will never forget the events that took place then. It is a lovely story.

Major General T.A. Richardson CB MBE

Editor's Notes: Concerning Heroes

For donkey's years now there has been a standing joke in our family regarding my Dad. It started around the mid-1950s when Dad took us on a touring holiday of Wales. As we approached the little coastal town of Towin he told us proudly, 'I was stationed here during the war!' After that, wherever we travelled in the British Isles, this phrase was repeated so many times that it became part of Davies folklore. When we were young my parents took my two brothers and I for holidays in various parts of the country. We are a very close family, and even though us lads now have our own families, it seemed natural to share holidays with Mum and Dad, with our children, and more recently with our grandchildren.

Even the very youngest have taken up the joke – as we drove through some remote village in Yorkshire, Norfolk, Suffolk, or Essex – almost anywhere – a little voice would pipe up mockingly, 'I was stationed here during the war!' Granddad, who was a great joker himself, would pretend to be embarrassed and give the offender a mock cuff round the ear, and it very often turned out that indeed he was stationed at that particular place during the war!

Although he is no longer with us, the joke persists, along with many other Ron Davies-isms, and the phrase still gets trotted out wherever we travel around the country. But the humour is gentle, and serves to give us an affectionate reminder of our dear old Dad, much loved, who to us was nothing short of a hero. There are four definitions of the word 'hero' in my dog-eared copy of the *Oxford English Dictionary*. Thinking about it, I guess that they could all apply to my Dad. As a child, I certainly believed that he was 'a man of superhuman qualities', not far short of Superman or Captain Marvel, who were the fictional heroes of my youth.

The next definition is 'illustrious warrior – as applied to heroes returning from battle.' Could anyone deny that this is supremely accurate when applied to Ron 'Popeye' Davies and his comrades in the Essex Yeomanry, and all the other veterans of D-Day?

After reading and re-reading his memoirs several times, I would submit that he was indeed 'a man admired for his achievements and noble qualities.' Again, it is a description that applies equally to his fellow heroes in the Armed Forces. Although, I have to say with a son's bias, that this definition applied to my Dad throughout his life.

The fourth definition is 'the chief male character in poem, play, or story.' As he had trod the boards of the amateur stage in the guise of 'Tevye', 'Billy Bigelow', 'Prince Sou-Chong', 'Lieutenant Fairfax', and 'The King of Siam', to mention but a few, this is indeed most appropriate to our Ron. So there you have it. My Dad – my hero!

I find it difficult to put into words exactly what it has meant to me to refine and edit *One Man's War*. In many ways it has kept my Dad alive for me. I feel as if I have lived all those amazing experiences with him, or as if he has patiently and lovingly conducted me through those momentous years of his life. I saw in vivid detail through his eyes the full horror of war, the extraordinary bravery of ordinary men, and that dogged humour in adversity that seems to be a quality inherent in the British.

I am blessed with a long memory, and the incident in chapter sixteen, when Ron jumped ship on 5 June 1944 to come home for what he thought might be his last reunion with his beloved Lily, is clearly imprinted on my mind. You might find this surprising considering that I was just four, but I have several other memories of incidents around that time and earlier, including doodle-bugs, air raids and running into the street outside my grandmother's house in Green Street to watch a dogfight between a German fighter and a Spitfire. I digress – back to 4 June. I remember this huge man in full uniform, complete with backpack and rifle, with my poor Mum clinging on to him, begging him not to go back. I also remember how bitterly she wept when he had gone, with me trying to comfort her.

My brothers and I were thrilled when Dad received letters from Greta and Alfred Plönes (chapter twenty-two) after the war; he read them out to us and showed us the photographs of them and their children. He told us that one day he would take us to meet them. I often looked forward to meeting those beautiful blond Dutch children. Alas, in those days, travel abroad was a prerogative of the better-off. By the time we actually got round to it the only ones still alive were Betsjie and Chrisjie, who were by then in their sixties. Nonetheless, it was a wonderful and loving reunion, one of the highlights of my life.

Throughout these memoirs Dad displays undisguised contempt for the American forces. This was based on certain incidents that he vividly describes,

Ron outside 13 Plataanstrasse, 1999. By Bill Davies.

when some of his comrades were killed or injured by so-called 'friendly fire'. Conscious of the historical fact that our American allies suffered great losses to help us free Europe from the Nazi death-grip, I did consider omitting some of these references for fear of causing offence, but of course this would have been presumptuous of me. These are Dad's experiences and thoughts, and so I have stuck simply to corrections in grammar, spelling and syntax, with a little additional detail gleaned from Mum's memory and from my discussions with Dad after he first showed me his manuscript.

Another great joy for me has been Dad's re-establishment of contact with the Essex Yeomanry. In the early 1990s Dad's sister, Betty, who lives in Harlow, saw a letter in one of her local newspapers appealing for any veterans of D-Day who had served with the regiment to attend a reunion. She contacted Dad, and he attended regular reunions for the rest of his life.

I was thrilled when Dad first took me as his guest to one of the reunions, which took place at the Marks Tey Hotel. I was amused when one of the elderly gentlemen pointed to me and whispered to his companions, 'Look! That's old Popeye's lad!' Popeye's lad? I was in my sixties!

Having listened to Dad's war stories as a boy, I knew many of the names and I was particularly pleased to meet Les Pratt. Dad had told me so many times that he had been in the Army with Boris Karloff's cousin, and there was this dapper, white-haired old gentleman, with a neatly trimmed moustache, the spitting image of his illustrious relative! It was also a very great privilege to meet Major General Tony Richardson and Colonel Dick Gosling, who features in this book. Sadly, like so many of these wonderful old soldiers, Les has since passed away, but his son Michael does valuable work in organising the reunion dinners at Harlow. I was also astonished to find that Gunner Harry Baker, another of Dad's old comrades, lives just a few hundred yards away from my wife and I in Frinton. We have become good friends, and intend to share future journeys to Harlow.

My brother Steve recently described our Dad as 'an inveterate story-teller'. He is right – this was one of many of Dad's unique qualities, and this is displayed to full effect in these pages. If nothing else, it is a damn good read; it will make you laugh and cry, and it should make you proud. I am sure that the thoughts he so generously shares with us were typical of the other young men who fought and died for the freedom we now enjoy. It has been a privilege for me to become acquainted with some of them, through my long immersion in these pages. I have always thought of them and my dear Dad as heroes, and my involvement in this project only confirms what I already knew.

Bill Davies

ONE MAN'S WAR.

...s 1936 and I was just turned sixteen, I had given up singing in the
...MES'S CHURCH CHOIR and I was no longer caddying at CREW'S HILL GOLF CLUB
...one day I met a mate of mine and he was in uniform and so I asked him if
...d joined the Army, but he said that he was in the TERRITORIAL ARMY, and he
...ased at WALTHAM CROSS. So I arranged to go with him on his next parade a
...up. I was told that I would have to get my father's permission which I ...
...no trouble. And so I joined up, but as I was under age I could only join
...OY'S SERVICE. I was now BOY DAVIES..2044166. I was issued with a unifor...
...s the old FIRST WORLD WAR uniform with knee length puttees and a wide
...ng belt with a bayonet frog attached. I had a peaked cap and the peak can...
...just above my eyes and the first time I wore it I thought I was the cat'...
...er's! I was also issued with an eighteen inch bayonet in a black
...ard, and I sat indoors and polished it up until it shone like a black
...nd, but the trouble was I had polished it with boot polish and when I
...d up on my next parade and we were inspected the officer pointed out the
...: marks on my trousers where the polish had rubbed off, but as I was a new
...it he let me off. We did two parades a week for which we received 1/6d,
...sometimes we went on a week-end camp and for that we got 3/-.The camp we
...at week-ends was at LIPPET'S HILL where the POLICE HELICOPTER BASE is at
...resent. We also had a yearly camp for a fortnight, which was at MANSTON i...

If we attended all the parades and the summer camp we got a BOUNTY of
...Y POUNDS. The Regiment was the 109th REGIMENT of the ROYAL ENGINEERS a...
...ask was to surround LONDON with search-lights in the event of a war.
...earch-light was a huge great thing and it was towed by a three ton lorr...
... was a TILLING-STEVENS petrol electric and it had solid tyres and when ...
...away at week-end camp I got my first taste of driving. It was fairly ea...
...se there were only two gears, forward and reverse, it was great fun.
... put on the sound locator and the idea was that we would listen through
...eadphones for the sound of an enemy aircraft and when we thought that it
...pot on we would shout "STRIKE ARC!" and in theory the search-light would
... up the aircraft, but of course it didn't always work, we didn't have RAD...
...ose days. In 1937 I had my seventeenth birthday and so I now became
...R R.A.DAVIES 2044166. On NOVEMBER the 11th that year we attended an
...TICE service at WALTHAM ABBEY and we were to march to the ABBEY from our
... hall in ELEANOR CROSS ROAD, with our regimental band leading the way,
...ur marching pace was fairly fast, so off we went marching very smartly
...s we approached the ABBEY, suddenly from down SUN STREET came the
...TION ARMY and their band was playing COME AND JOIN US and of course the
...empo's clashed and we were tripping over our feet trying to keep in ste...

The first page of Ron's original typescript. Courtesy of Mrs L. Davies.

Notes on the Text

There are a few references in Dad's manuscript which are not borne out by recorded history. I have marked these clearly in the narrative. I have been trying to resolve these inconsistencies through research; my findings, such as they are, are as follows:

Page 63: Regimental history shows that the SPs supplied were initially Howitzer Priests with 105mm guns. These were replaced by the Canadian Sextons in March 1944.

The young man who drowned at Lynmouth was Lieutenant F.H. McKaskie, who is listed on the Regimental Roll of Honour. He and Sergeant Wilson were demonstrating disembarkation in full kit; they swam out to the breakwater, but both got into difficulties while returning to shore. The Sergeant was rescued, but tragically the young officer drowned. He was only twenty-one. Thanks to General Richardson and Bill Coyston for their assistance in revealing this.

Page 87: Bill Wilby survived the war; in fact, General Richardson saw him as recently as 1992. I can only surmise that Dad was confusing Bill with another tank commander. I spoke to Colonel A.R. Motion on the General's advice, and he said he remembered that Bill had been injured, so that may have been the reason for Dad taking charge temporarily.

Page 93: The rescuing officer could not have been Dick Gosling. I spoke to Colonel Gosling and General Richardson, who advised me that Dick was injured on D-Day and sent back to England for medical treatment. In *Gold Beach Jig* by Tim Saunders, the following excerpt from the diary of Colonel (then Major) Gosling is published:

> … a swarm of angry bees buzzed just over our heads; our Hampshire comrades, war experienced, recognised German heavy machine gun fire and

ran forward. In front of us the sand furrowed and spurted from Spandaus firing down the beach in enfilade on fixed lines from Le Hamel. The Colonel shouted to us to lie down, but the wet sand was unattractive, so we sprinted for the cover of the dunes fifty yards ahead.

Some mortar bombs and 88mm shells were falling and one of the former landed just behind the CO and I, smashing one of his arms and filling my leg with shell fragments. We managed to make it to the dunes and flung ourselves in a depression in the sand. Intermittent bombs and shells continued to fall and machine gun fire swarmed through the reeds above our heads. We laid very flat and still – after a few minutes, German fire seemed to have switched down to the beach again (to engage another flight of landing craft) and I crawled up the dune to peer over the other side. Horrified to see a German twenty yards away, I fired my revolver in his general direction and hastily slid back. A Hampshire Corporal lying near me, already wounded, knelt up to look over the dune and was at once shot through the chest by a sniper.

Colonel Motion said he thought that there was a tank disabled on the beach, and that he thought that Sergeant 'Ozzie' Avis had picked up the crew some days later. He gave me Sergeant Avis' telephone number, and I had a chat with the Sergeant, who lives in Colchester. My hopes were dashed when he told me that the tank commander whose crew he picked up was a lieutenant, and that in any event, Popeye Davies was Gunner in an SP. My sources exhausted, I shall just have to let the matter remain a mystery. My Dad started to write his account of his experiences in the late 1980s, some forty-odd years after the end of the war, so perhaps it is not surprising if one or two memories are a little hazy. Dear old Colonel Gosling, who remembers Dad for his singing, advised me not to worry. He said that the account should be accepted as Dad's personal memories. Good advice!

Page 103: Private Ned Spry, who according to Dad was killed in the same incident as Ralph Diamond, is not mentioned on the official Roll of Honour, published in Captain Gee's *History of the Essex Yeomanry*. Colonel Motion remembers the incident, and also recollects Ned Spry. He thought it was possible that Ned had been killed, but the Roll of Honour would surely have recorded his death. Perhaps Ned was injured, possibly badly. Again, there are so few veterans left who might clarify the situation, and these gentlemen are being asked to cast their minds back sixty years! So forgive me – this mystery will have to remain unexplained.

Page 107: There is no record of an officer named J. Savage – not on the Roll of Officers, nor on the Roll of Honour. The officer in question could have been either Lieutenant Sayer of 511 Battery or Lieutenant Hicks of 413 Battery.

My thanks go to General Richardson, Colonel Gosling, Colonel Motion, Sergeant Avis, Colonel Warburton, Bill Coyston and good old Harry Baker, all of whom have graciously shared their memories with me. I regret to advise that Colonel Motion and Colonel Warburton passed away during the run-up to publication.

1

Born Between the Wars

I was born on 2 October 1920, two years after the end of the supposed war to end all wars. My father fought in that conflict, so I suppose it gave us a special affinity. Him, myself, and most of my brothers – successive generations fighting for King and Country.

My father Walter had a very unhappy childhood, losing his father before he had a chance to get to know him. My grandfather William was a master builder in Wales, and had been fairly comfortably off, but in 1898, when Dad was only a month or two old, his father died of a heart attack aged thirty-two.

His mother Marion remarried a few years later. Her second husband Edgar Barton was a medical student, but not long after the wedding he was knocked down by a tram. This left him permanently blind, and the psychological effects left him with an uncontrollable temper. His little stepson became the butt of his bad temper, and Dad was regularly beaten. When his stepbrother, Arthur, was born, Dad was relegated to second best. Arthur was the apple of his father's eye – care and attention was lavished on him, he received the best education, and was sent to college.

At fourteen my father decided that he had had enough, and he ran away from home. He went to live with his maternal grandparents, Mr and Mrs Brown, in Welshpool. After a while he unofficially adopted their name and called himself Walter Brown, although he obviously reverted to Davies at some later stage.

He went to work for an engineering company and took an apprenticeship in tool-making. It was 1914, and the Great War had begun, so there was plenty of work for the company. After a couple of years he became old enough for military service and he joined the Royal Army Medical Corps. He was sent into the trenches in France as a stretcher-bearer.

Gas attacks were frequent, and unfortunately he became a victim. As a result he suffered damage to his left eye, and contracted rheumatic fever. He was invalided out with a small pension after having spent some time at a hospital in Canterbury to recuperate.

It was in Canterbury that he became a Salvationist, and every Sunday he went to service at the local Salvation Army Citadel. It was there that he met my mother, who rejoiced in the names of Winifred Alice May Letitia Henrietta Amanda Vera Violet Mabel Bushell. This is something I have always remembered, and I think it is worth recording.

Mum was born in Fordwych, just outside of Canterbury, and was the youngest child of her mother's second marriage. Her father was killed in the Boer War, and her stepfather and six of her brothers were killed in the Great War. They became engaged and were married in 1919, and went to live in Birmingham where Dad obtained a job with a firm called Lucas. My Mum's brother, Jack, also worked there.

Mum and Dad carried on with their Salvation Army activities, and Dad learned to play the euphonium. He had always been very musical; he had a fine tenor voice, and could also play the concertina. They lived at 33 Barr Street in Hockley, a suburb of Birmingham, and it was there that little Ronnie was born! Apparently I weighed ten pounds, and it was something of a difficult birth. Two years later my sister Joyce was born.

Around that time work became very scarce, and Dad became redundant. Try as he may he could not find work, and before long they couldn't pay the rent. No such thing as job seeker's allowance in those days! So the four of us went to live with Granny Bushell in Canterbury. It was only a little old two-up, two-down cottage, so God knows how they managed.

After a while they managed to get a cottage of their own in a village called Charterham. Dad still couldn't find work, and one day he borrowed sixpence from Granny Bushell and did an accumulator on the horses. Their luck was in because he won seventeen pounds! That was a small fortune to them, and it kept them going for weeks. Of course, it ran out eventually, and before long they were once again stony broke.

One day Dad heard about a job going with a concert party in Ramsgate. The problem was, how to get there for the audition? They couldn't afford to go by train or bus, so they decided to walk. I still find it difficult to understand how they did it. They just piled all their belongings into baby Joyce's pram, and set out to walk from Canterbury to Ramsgate. I don't know how far it was, but one of my earliest memories is of being carried on my Dad's shoulders on that journey. When we arrived at Ramsgate Dad found a lodging house run by a Mr and Mrs Taverner, and the next day he had his audition and got the job!

For a while, everything went smoothly. The house was quite big, and our landlords gave Mum a job as a cook. Dad worked for 'The Fol-de-Rols', who performed on the beach.

The Taverners had a son whose name was Dickie. He was about twelve, and he took young Ronnie under his wing. I had some wonderful adventures with him. There were not many buses around in those days; instead, we travelled on the Penny Brake. This was a bit like a double-decker bus, pulled by two horses. One of these went from Ramsgate to Pegwell Bay, and I remember going there several times with Dickie Taverner. We took with us a large laundry basket. We went when the tide was out, and waded out for hundreds of yards. Dickie showed me how to put my hands down under the sand to catch great big crabs and small flatfish called dabs. I remember that we used to fill the basket almost to the top, and then go home on the Brake. We would give the catch to my Mum, and she would cook them and prepare them for the guests. She was very good at dressing a crab. A dab hand you might say! She used to make them look so appetizing, and although I was not yet five, I can remember being so proud just to be a part of it all.

Before long my brother Dennis was born, and the Taverners couldn't put us up any more. We found a nice little house to rent in the same street, 10 Rodney Street. Mum continued to work for the Taverners, and Dad carried on with the 'Fol-de-Rols'.

Of course, the concert party was seasonal, and so come winter Dad was out of work. As I mentioned earlier, Dad was good on the concertina, and by this time he had acquired three. One was large, one was medium, and one was tiny! His speciality was to play a version of 'The Bells of St Mary's' using all three – I can remember how the music filled the house when he practiced at home.

Anyway, he was wondering how to make a living during the winter, and one of his mates in the concert party suggested that he try busking – playing outside public houses, and to theatre and cinema queues etc. Dad wasn't sure about this, so he went to the police station to find out if it was legal. They said that it was, so long as he obeyed the rules. For instance, if he was playing outside a pub he could only put one foot inside the door, or if he was playing in the street he could only put one foot on the kerb. He decided to give it a try, and that evening we went up to a pub in Yorke Street. Mum had Joyce in a pram, and we stood outside the beer garden while Dad played and sang. In no time at all we had a hat full of coppers. We went home and sat around the kitchen table counting it, and there was just over ten shillings.

So, for a while, Dad became a busker in the winter, and a 'Fol-de-Rol' in the summer, but it was too good to last. The following year the 'Fol-de-Rols' went broke, so once again Dad was unemployed. He carried on busking full-time, and I remember following him along the beach as he sang all the popular songs of that time. He did very well, and made quite a good living. As with many entertainers of the day, he used to black up using burned cork.

Later on that year my brother Wally was born, and my Mum had a very difficult time. I remember how she screamed, so much that Joyce and I hid under our bed with our hands over our ears. The new baby weighed only three pounds, and for a while it was touch and go as to whether he would survive, but thank goodness, he did! So, now there were four kids, and we were all sleeping in the same bed!

The year was 1926, and the General Strike was on, and as a result the busking wasn't paying very well. People just didn't have the money. I had started school, very reluctantly! I remember crying my eyes out when Mum first took me, but I soon got used to it.

There is one incident from that time that sticks in my mind. You didn't see many aeroplanes, so when one flew over, it was quite an event. They were mostly biplanes, and we would stand and watch them in wonder. One day a flying boat came over, and we were absolutely agog. It circled lower and lower and landed in the sea, just outside the harbour. We ran like mad down to the harbour, because we wanted to see the pilot. We lined up all along the harbour wall, craning our necks as a small boat went out to fetch the crew. They came back and tied up right underneath where we were standing, so I had to lean right over to see them. The boys behind me also leaned over, and someone started pushing. The next thing I knew I was plunging into the water. I couldn't swim, but one of the boatmen fished me out with a boat-hook. Someone wrapped me up in a blanket, and I was carried back home. Mum ticked me off, and then she made us all a hot cup of cocoa.

There was some relief when the General Strike was over, but life was still hard. There were still more men than ever out of work, and money was scarce. Dad wasn't earning much out of busking, partly because people didn't have the money to give, and because more and more men were turning to busking to earn a living. So Dad decided to try his luck in London. Granny Barton, Dad's mother, had taken over a shop in Ponders End High Street in Enfield. She was an agent for the Singer Sewing Machine Company, and she ran the shop while Mr Barton carried out the repairs in the workshop at the back of the premises. This was quite remarkable when you consider his disability.

2

The Move to Enfield

Dad decided as a matter of expediency to mend his fences with his mother and stepfather, and he wrote a letter asking his mother if she could find us a place in Enfield. I don't know quite how she arranged it, but eventually we were offered a council house near to Granny and Mr Barton.

And so we moved from our lovely house by the seaside in Ramsgate to Enfield in Middlesex. Our house was a nice three-bedroomed property, 10 Ashley Road. It was just down Green Street, a mile or so away from Granny Barton. In those days Enfield was just a small country town, nothing like it is today. We were delighted with the house – it was very spacious. There was no electricity; everything was gas, even the lights.

In the front room we had what was called a Kitchener, which was essentially a fireplace with an oven and hobs on top. All the cooking was done there, and at the back of the house there was a scullery where Mum did the washing, with hot water provided by a big solid-fuel boiler. There was an old-fashioned butler sink with just a cold water tap. There was a separate bathroom, with a proper plumbed-in bath! That also had only a cold water tap, so Mum used to boil water in the scullery and carry it through to the bathroom in buckets. After a few months we had a hot water geyser installed, and we thought that was the height of luxury! It certainly beat the way we had to bathe before we moved there. It had always been in the old tin bath in front of the fire.

To save on the gas bill we all went to bed with a candle, and during the evening, before bed time, Mum would take a shovelful of hot embers from the Kitchener to start a fire in our bedrooms – it was the only form of heating we had. Of course the ashes had to be cleared away the next morning. We also had an old-fashioned bed-warmer; it was a copper pan on a long handle, and was designed to be filled with warm ashes or embers, but Mum used hot water. It just about took the chill off before we got into bed.

The garden was huge; there were two apple trees and a pear tree. Along the fence on one side grew loganberries and blackberries, and on the other side there were rows of gooseberries. The area nearest the house was mainly grass, but at the bottom of the garden Mum and Dad created a vegetable patch. I remember that one of my chores was to go down the garden to dig up potatoes, carrots, onions, and cabbages etc for our dinner. Mum encouraged us boys to cultivate our own little patch, which caused a few arguments! We each had different ideas on what we wanted to grow. Boys being boys, we wanted to play, so we hung a swing on one of the apple trees, and we had lots of fun in our own private playground. Joyce joined in all of our games; we never really thought about her as a girl. I guess in those days she was just one of the boys!

Dad took up busking full-time and was quite successful at it. He went up to central London to play outside all the big theatres and cinemas. Unfortunately, it meant that he was usually out all day and very often came home after us kids had gone to bed. As a result we didn't get to spend a lot of time with him, and when he was home he was often too tired to play. This was a shame, because he could be a lot of fun. He was an excellent swimmer, and taught all of us boys, and we became sufficiently proficient for Mum to allow us to go down to the River Lea by ourselves. Big brother Ronnie was made responsible for looking after all of the others. We spent many happy hours swimming there; we found a place where water was discharged from the North Met Power Station and this had the effect of warming up that whole stretch of river. I remember one time we were down there when somebody stole all of our clothes. We had to walk home wearing just our old woollen bathing costumes.

We also used to swim under a big railway bridge that we called the Seven Arches, and in a tributary of the river that was known as 'The Cut'. Our swimming trips there came to an abrupt end when there was a tragic accident involving a lad whose name was Frankie Hepburn. There were safe places to swim, and other places where underwater weeds could tangle around your legs and pull you down. One of these places was straddled by a large water pipe, about three feet in diameter. It was painted black, and went right across the river which was about fifteen feet across at that point. We often used to walk across the pipe for a dare, but poor Frankie slipped and fell, and disappeared under the water. Some of us jumped in to look for him, but we couldn't find him. Someone ran for help and after a couple of hours he was found. I'll never forget the anguish I felt, walking up Green Street behind the cart which carried his body.

The police put up a notice banning swimming in The Cut, but we still carried on swimming by the power station. It was there that I met Ned and

Harry Hussey. They were both fantastic swimmers, and we formed a friendship that was to last all our lives. Little did I know then that we would end up as brothers-in-law.

When I was about nine, Dad started to take me with him when he went busking. When I wasn't at school that is. My job was to be the 'Bottle Man'. The bottle was a velvet bag which Mum had made. It was fixed to the end of a long cane, and when we played to a cinema or theatre queue it was my task to go along the queue, gathering coppers. When I think about it I guess that Dad had the idea that having a little boy to do the bottling would attract more cash, and he was right! We used to do pretty well. Dad had teamed up with two other musicians – Eddie Hollies on trumpet, and Bert Hyde on banjo. Dad did the singing, in those days he had a lovely tenor voice. He was now playing the piano-accordion, and they were quite an accomplished little trio. I enjoyed these outings immensely, and I wouldn't be surprised if this was where I got the taste for performing and stage work.

After a while Dad started to get us a few gigs at the local working men's clubs. To my delight he taught me to sing, and I went on stage to perform with the group. Dad would black me up, and we were billed as 'Uncle Wally and Sambo' singing all the popular black minstrel songs. We really went down well. We performed at various working men's clubs, Enfield, Ponders End, and Edmonton among others. This happy little phase of my life ceased when Mum became worried that I was under age, and she put a stop to it.

Mum became pregnant again, and along came brother Tony. He weighed twelve pounds when he was born, and my poor Mum had a terrible time. What with this, and things in general, she was not at all well, and nor was Dad. He had started having blackouts, probably brought on by the gas attacks he had suffered during the war. Very often he was brought home by the boys in the band, and sometimes by the police, and he appeared to be getting worse. When Tony was just a few months old, Dad was taken into hospital after a suspected heart attack, and shortly afterwards, to our horror, Mum went to hospital too! So, there we were, four kids with me the oldest at ten, and no one to look after us.

Our Granny Bushell, who by then had left Canterbury to live with her other daughter, Carrie, in Liverpool, came down to Enfield to take care of us. The poor old dear found that she just couldn't cope. I daresay we were a bit of a handful. So, someone, I don't know who, decided that me and Joyce being the two oldest should be temporarily taken into care.

I can't remember where Joyce was taken, but the awful memory of the orphanage in Parkstone where I was sent will always be with me. What a terrible place! It was near Poole in Dorset, and all of us boys there were treated abominably. We were forced to take showers (unheard of at home!) and as we ran out of the cold stone shower room there was a master standing at the door with a long cane. This sadistic so-and-so took great delight in whacking each one of us on our bare bottoms as we went past. After six weeks I was in absolute despair, there seemed to be no end to the terror. Then one day I was summoned to the Headmaster's study. I thought that I was in trouble, so it was with fear and trembling that I opened the door. To my complete surprise, I was faced with the ample figure of my Aunt Carrie! Even though she had a face like thunder, I almost wept with relief. Let me describe Aunt Carrie to you. She was my Mum's eldest sister, and by any standards she was a formidable woman. You crossed her at your peril. She wasn't very tall, about five feet six inches, but she could only be described as big. She had muscular forearms, and was one of those ladies who, when faced with confrontation, would mime rolling up her sleeves and spitting on her hands. She ran a seaman's café in Liverpool, and kept a policeman's truncheon under the counter in case of trouble. Many a drunken sailor got his skull cracked as a result, and she had built up a fearsome reputation. This was the avenging angel that I was faced with! She grabbed me by the ear, and dragged me out of that horrible place, out through the gates, and then pushed me into a taxi that she had waiting. I yelled all the way because I felt that at any moment my ear would become detached from my head!

She didn't say a word until we were on the train heading north. Then she cried, and hugged me. She held me tight for the whole journey. When we arrived at her house in Liverpool Joyce was already there, having been previously rescued. We stayed with Aunt Carrie for more than six months, and they were very happy days. It was a big house; three storeys high, and the café was in the cellar. It was called 'The Olde Supper Cellar' and was in Kempston Street near Liverpool Docks.

In 1930 Liverpool was teeming with seafarers. Aunt Carrie's customers came from all over the world. There were British sailors, foreign sailors, ship's officers, lascars, dockers; they all had tales to tell, and I can tell you it was all fascinating for a young lad. The café was very popular, the regulars used to call Aunt Carrie 'Ma Robinson' and they all loved her cooking. Mind you she wouldn't stand any nonsense, she ruled with a rod of iron. She didn't allow bad language or horse-play, and as I mentioned earlier, she was not frightened to use the truncheon.

Us kids were not allowed in the cellar after six pm, but the house was huge – Joyce and I had some wonderful adventures exploring it. There were two of my cousins living there, Bob and Bill. Bob was married, and his wife Winifred worked in the café. They had a daughter whose name escapes me, and she was our self-appointed guardian angel. She wasn't much older than us, but she was as tough as old boots, and she wouldn't let the local kids bully us. There was a huge Irish community in Liverpool, and there was always trouble between the Catholics and the Protestants. We often used to play in Sefton Park, and we stood out from the other kids because we wore shoes! As soon as they heard our southern accent we became targets, and the first thing they would ask is 'Are you Catholic or Protestant?' We had no way of knowing of which denomination our tormentors were, so there was every chance of getting a beating, but our little angel used to look after us, and often sent these boys on their way with a flea in their ear. Joyce and I didn't take long to toughen up, and we learned how to defend ourselves.

Both the Green and Orange Lodges organised parades and processions, and they were magnificent affairs. The Lodge men wore splendid costumes, and were accompanied by large brass bands. There was one in particular that I recall, it was an Orange Lodge Parade, and was led by a young boy dressed as William of Orange, riding on a beautiful white horse.

All the processions went past our house, but we could only watch from inside. It was far too dangerous to go out into the street. They came down Kempston Street, turned right into Moss Street, and then left into London Road. The rival Lodge would lay in wait on the corner, and pelt the procession with stones and bad fruit. Fighting inevitably broke out, and I remember seeing mounted police riding up Kempston Street line abreast, lashing out with their riot batons, and knocking people to the ground.

Aunt Carrie was a widow, but she enjoyed male company. She had a number of men friends, who we were instructed to call 'uncle'. One of them was Uncle Jock. He was the skipper of a cargo ship so he was only there for short periods, but he happened to be there at the same time as us. He was a big Scotsman, and he was great fun except when he was drunk. When he was, we were terrified of him! Cousin Bill and I slept in the attic, and one night after we had blown out the candle, a light appeared under the door. It burst open and the huge figure of Uncle Jock appeared, cursing and swearing. From where I lay he appeared at least ten feet tall, and I hid under the covers until Bill (who was grown up) led the old boy unprotesting back to his room.

As soon as Uncle Jock went back to sea, another 'uncle' took his place. This time it was Uncle Bluey. He was a ship's butcher, and he was also a very big man. I can picture his ruddy complexion, and his very large red nose. He would perform feats of strength to amuse me, and one of his favourites was to remove the crown cork from a bottle of pop without using an opener. He would then take it between his thumb and forefinger and bend it in half. I tried for years afterwards to copy him, but I have never been able to do it.

To counterbalance Aunt Carrie's strictness, we were spoilt by Granny Bushell. She was every young lad's dream of a grandmother. She had a wealth of fascinating stories, and an infectious laugh. I liked putting my hand on her ample tummy, because when she laughed it wobbled like a jelly. Granny had her own little corner behind the counter in the café, and whenever Aunt Carrie said no to my frequent requests for a bottle of pop, Granny would slip me one from under her apron, and I would stuff it up my jumper. Happy days indeed!

Sometimes on Saturday mornings Bill would take me to the Majestic Cinema. It was a penny to go in, and for that we saw two films (silent of course) and after the films had finished the pianist would invite the audience to have a sing-song. We were also given a complimentary bag of sweets!

Bill and Bob were both blacksmiths, and they had been working on the construction of the brand-new Mersey Tunnel. The grand opening was attended by King George the Fifth. Both my cousins were invited, and Bill took me with him on his motor-bike. I had a grandstand view, sitting on Bill's shoulders! Afterwards, we drove through the tunnel and back on the motor-bike. What an exciting day that was!

I loved it so much in Liverpool, our stay there seemed never-ending, but finally it was time to leave. Mum and Dad had both recovered from their respective illnesses, so Aunt Carrie and Granny Bushell took us back to Enfield. What a reunion that was! There were lots of tears, and hugs, and despite my love for my Aunt and my Granny, it was such a relief to be back with my family. I also had a new baby brother, Alan – he was a dear little soul! Aunt Carrie and Granny stayed for a couple of weeks and it was wonderful to have all the people I loved under one roof for a while.

3

Joining Up

I haven't said very much so far about my mother, so I shall devote the first few paragraphs of this chapter to her. She was a little shorter than Aunt Carrie, but she was very much cast in the same mould. She was a stout lady, tough, no nonsense, with the same muscular forearms. She was without doubt the best Mother that anyone could wish for. She was an excellent cook, and always made sure that we were fed well. She always said that her priorities were rent, food, and keeping warm.

In those days there were very few labour-saving devices, and she worked her fingers to the bone looking after her large family. You can imagine how much washing there was. She used a big old tin bath and a scrubbing board, and an old-fashioned mangle. All the kids would take it in turns to wind the handle.

Her routine was to get up at six am to clear the ashes from the fireplaces, upstairs and down; she then cleaned and black-leaded the Kitchener, the front door-step was red-leaded, and there were various other household chores. Then she would wake the children, prepare breakfast, and get us ready for school.

She was very strict with us, but at the same time she was very loving. She would give you a good hiding for some misdemeanour, and then give you a cuddle. She was full of fun, always singing, and whenever we had 'a bit of a do' she was always the life and soul of the party. She was very protective of us kids, and didn't hesitate to come to school and berate our teachers if she thought we had been treated unfairly. But heaven help you if you grumbled about some punishment meted out by the school and she found out you deserved it! That would earn you a hefty clip round the ear.

Mum had lots of funny little sayings. For instance, if visitors outstayed their welcome, she would yawn elaborately and say, 'Nearer the night the worse the weather, I'm at home and I wish that everybody else was!' On teaching us how to cross the road safely she would say, 'Look right, look left, look right again, and make sure nothing is coming. After all, you don't want to be dead for the rest of

Ron's Mum and Aunt Carrie, mid-1950s. Courtesy of Mrs L. Davies.

your life, do you?' I also remember her saying to me, 'If you fall out of that tree and break your leg, don't come running to me!'

As you've probably realised, Mum was very strong, in fact she was a match for most men. She wouldn't hesitate to have a go at anyone who annoyed her. One typical example was when a neighbour of ours abused her. His name was Eli, and he was quite a decent man when he was sober. He had been down to the pub, and had one or two pints too many. He staggered past our front gate while Mum and I were chatting to our next door neighbour. He leered at Mum and said, 'Hallo fatty!' Mum said, 'I've told you before Eli, don't call me fatty!' The silly man replied, 'OK fatty!' That was when Mum threw a perfect uppercut, right on his chin. He went down as if he had been pole-axed, and it took fifteen minutes to bring him round. Needless to say, he didn't ever call Mum names again.

Another time young Tony was playing outside, and was being bullied by an older boy. Even though Tony was the smaller of the two, he gave this boy a fourpenny one. The boy's mum, Biddy Green, came running out of her house, and clipped Tony round the ear. Unfortunately for her, our Mum happened to be watching, and she ran out into the street. Mrs Green saw her coming and legged it back to her front door. Mum caught up with her, and grabbed her by the scruff of the neck. The back of Mrs Green's dress was torn off, and Mum got her head in an arm-lock, and gave her a right pasting. I seem to remember that the police were involved, but I can't remember what happened after that.

She was one tough cookie was my Mum, but at the same time she was kind and loving, and there was nobody like her in the world. All my brothers and sisters will tell you the same.

The family wasn't complete yet. My youngest brother Colin was born in 1931. So he was eight when war broke out. He was evacuated with all those other poor little devils with labels around their necks. I think that was in 1942. Along with many other kids from homes in Central Avenue, he was sent to Southport in Lancashire. Unfortunately for Colin and his pal Bobby Trundle, the lady they were billeted with didn't know how to look after small children, and the long and short of it is that they ran away, and ended up with dear old Aunt Carrie in Liverpool. After an initial furore, they were allowed to stay with her in Liverpool until the end of the war. They had a few adventures there, similar to mine and Joyce's, but that is Colin's story.

Our baby sister Betty (christened Winifred) came along in 1936, and it was one of my regrets that I missed her early years. She was never evacuated, Mum keeping her baby daughter at home. Of course, at the time of Betty's birth the threat of war was looming, and she was still a baby when I joined the Territorial

Army. This is how it happened. I had been singing in the choir at St James Church in Enfield, but had to give it up when my voice broke. I had also recently stopped caddying at Crews Hill Golf Club. So, I suppose I was at a bit of a loose end. One day, shortly after my sixteenth birthday, I met a mate of mine in the street, and he was in uniform. I asked him if he had joined the Army, and he told me it was the Territorials. It was the 109th Regiment of the Royal Engineers, and was based at Waltham Cross in Hertfordshire, which wasn't far from where I lived. Well, I really fancied myself in that uniform, so I asked if I could go with him on his next parade. He willingly agreed, and so I went along. The sergeant told me I would have to get my father's permission before I could join up. Dad had no objections. In fact he encouraged me to join. And so I became BOY DAVIES 2044166. Under-age recruits had to join the Boys Service.

I was issued with an old First World War uniform, with knee-length puttees and a wide webbing belt with a bayonet frog attached. I had a peaked cap, and the peak came down to just above my eyes. The first time I wore it, I thought I was the cat's whiskers! I was also issued with an eighteen-inch bayonet in a black scabbard, and I sat indoors and polished it up until it shone like a black diamond. Knowing no better, I had used boot polish, and when I was inspected

Ron's mother. Courtesy of Mrs L. Davies.

at the next parade, the officer pointed out the black marks on my trousers where the polish had rubbed off. I must have looked a bit crestfallen, so he let me off as I was a new recruit.

We attended two parades a week, for which we received one and sixpence, and sometimes we went on a weekend camp for which we received three shillings. The weekend camp was at Lippett's Hill in Epping Forest, on the site of what is now the Metropolitan Police helicopter base. We also went to a fortnight's camp once a year at Manston in Kent. If we attended every parade and the annual camp, we received a bonus of thirty pounds.

The Regiment's task was to surround London with searchlights in the event of war. The one we used was a huge great thing, it was towed by a Tilling-Stevens lorry. The Tilling-Stevens was a three-tonner, a petrol-electric, and it had solid tyres. When we were at camp I got my first taste of driving. It was fairly easy, because there were only two gears – forward and reverse – it was great fun.

I was put on the sound locator. The idea was that we would listen through our headphones for the sound of an enemy aircraft, and when we thought that it was spot on, we would shout 'Strike arc!' and in theory, the searchlight would light up the aircraft. Needless to say, it didn't always work, but it was all we had. No such thing as Radar in those days.

When I reached my seventeenth birthday I became SAPPER R.A. DAVIES 2044166. I remember the Armistice Day service at Waltham Abbey on 11 November that year. We were to march to the Abbey from our drill hall in Eleanor Cross Road, with our regimental band leading the way. Our marching pace was fairly fast, so off we went, marching very smartly, and as we approached the Abbey, suddenly from down Sun Street came the Salvation Army. Their band was playing 'Come and Join Us' at a completely different tempo, so of course the rhythms clashed. We were all tripping over our feet trying to keep in step!

In 1938 it looked almost certain that there would be a war, and when Chamberlain went to Munich to negotiate peace with Hitler, the Territorial Army was placed on alert. We went down to Ingatstone in Essex and set up a searchlight site. While we were there we had a few practice runs with a real aircraft, and on at least one occasion we actually managed to light one up.

Shortly after the 1938 crisis the 109th were disbanded, and we were given the option of signing off or joining another Territorial unit, the Essex Yeomanry. So, not wanting to sign off, I became YEOMAN R.A. DAVIES.

The Yeomanry was formed back in the dim distant past by gentlemen farmers. They banded together, supplied their own horses and weapons, and offered their services to the Crown. Just before the First World War, they formed the

Territorial Army. The Essex Yeomanry at this time was the 147th Regiment of the Royal Horse Artillery, but only the officers had horses.

I was in 431 Battery, commanded by Major J. Todhunter. Some of our lads had originally been part of a group started at the Murex factory in Waltham Cross, and others had come from the Territorials based at Harlow. We were supposed to be mechanised, but although we had guns, there were no vehicles to tow them with. When we did need to tow them we hired sand and ballast lorries from a local company called Crows. The guns were 1917-vintage eighteen-pounders, and printed in large words down each barrel was the direction, 'FOR DRILL PURPOSES ONLY'. All we could do was to go through the motions, we never did get to fire them. Around June 1939 we were equipped with a later version of the eighteen-pounder, and you can imagine our excitement when we went off to Larkhill Barracks on Salisbury Plain for our annual camp, and actually got to fire them. They had a terrific crack when they went off, but it was just a matter of getting used to them. They were made obsolete two months later!

4

Lily and Me

About the time I was at Ingatstone with the searchlight, I wrote to my pal Ned Hussey, and asked him to fix up a date for me with his young sister Lily. Ned was courting my sister Joyce at the time. I had met Lily once or twice, she was sweet seventeen, and pretty as a picture. I hadn't got the nerve to ask her out directly, so I took the easy way out. Anyway, she said yes, and we started to go out together. Our idea of a posh night out was to walk to the local flea-pit (The

Ron with his rifle. Courtesy of Mrs L. Davies.

Premier Cinema in Enfield Highway) and get some fish and chips afterwards. We would eat the fish and chips out of newspaper as we walked home.

What can I say? I was absolutely head over heels in love. Young though we were, we knew we were soulmates. By this time I was in the real army, and was stationed at Newmarket. I got away as often as I could, and when I was home, Lily and I were together constantly.

We used to dream about having our own house, and starting a little family. We knew it wouldn't be easy, my job didn't pay very much, and I wasn't able to save an awful lot, because my Mum desperately needed the house-keeping money. Lily was pretty much in the same boat.

Our families became very close, what with Lily and me and Ned and Joyce always round each other's houses, and it wasn't long before we were in effect just one big family. In fact, after the war our Colin married Lily's youngest sister Marjie, so then there were three marriages within the two families. Must be some kind of record!

With war looming on the horizon we knew that the day would come when I would have to go off and fight. We also knew that there was a possibility that I wouldn't come back. So, we decided to get married. When I look back, I think, 'blimey, we were only babies'. Still, you had to grow up fast in those days.

We got engaged, and the date was set for 4 November 1939. I managed to get a weekend pass, and several of my mates from the Regiment came with me to form a Guard of Honour. I was in full dress uniform, peaked cap, leather Sam Browne belt, and leather riding boots (highly polished of course!) And to top it off, a pair of spurs. They jingled as I walked, and brother, did I feel full of swank! As I got off the bus at Carter Hatch Lane I passed my little brothers, Tony, Alan, and Colin, who were on their way to the cinema for the afternoon. I can't quite remember why, I guess that Mum felt they weren't old enough to attend the actual service, although they did attend the 'do' later. I stood and chatted to them for a while, and Colin, who was the youngest, was looking around at people passing by as if to say, 'look! This is my big brother the soldier!' I gave them a couple of coppers each for some sweets, and off they went.

The wedding was at St James Church, and for some reason I can remember that the vicar was wearing a pair of Wellington boots! I can only imagine that he had been officiating at a funeral earlier, and that he had been wearing the boots around the grave side. He had either forgotten that he was wearing them, or else he just couldn't be bothered to take them off. Lily was given away by her big brother Harry, because her dad had died in an accident when she was fourteen. As we walked out of the church, the Guard of Honour formed an arch.

Ron and Lily's wedding with both
grandmothers. Courtesy of Mrs L. Davies.

Lily with baby, 1941. Courtesy of
Mrs L. Davies.

They didn't have rifles or swords, so they used the swagger sticks that they were allowed to carry with dress uniform. The reception was held at Lily's mum's house at Bantam Close on the Carter Hatch Estate, just around the corner. We both had big families, and of course all my mates were there, and we had a great time. We started out with one barrel of beer, and I seem to recall that another barrel or two arrived some time during the evening. The blokes who brought them were complete strangers to me, but what the heck! We invited them in. Needless to say there were quite a few sore heads the next morning. We spent our wedding night at my Mum's house in Central Avenue, but alas, no time or money for a honeymoon! Early on the Sunday morning I was off with my pals to catch the train back to Newmarket.

So, there I was, married at nineteen. It was terrible having to leave her so soon. We were both heartbroken, but that was just how it was. We went on to have three smashing boys, but I'll tell you about that later.

5

The Onset of War

The Essex Yeomanry had been mobilised on 1 September. This was only two days before Britain declared war on Germany, after the Nazis invaded Poland. To be honest it didn't come as a surprise, it was really only a matter of time. We used to listen to the news on our old crystal set radio, and it was pretty clear which way it was going.

I was working in the Co-op Dairy in Enfield Highway at the time. I received a message while I was working to go home and pack my kit, and then I was picked up by, yes, you guessed it, a Crow's sand and ballast lorry! We were taken to the drill hall in Harlow, and because they had no beds for us at that time, we had to sleep on the floor. We slept on palliasses, or as we called them, friendly donkeys. They were filled with straw, and it took a lot of getting used to.

Each day we would be marched along the road to Harlow Mill for our meals. We had an old sergeant named Jack Gilbert, he had a voice like a fog-horn, and when he shouted 'LEFT-RIGHT-LEFT-RIGHT', it sounded more like a roar from a wounded bear. As we marched along we took the mickey out of him, and as he shouted 'LEFT-RIGHT' we shouted 'WOOF-WOOF!' It went like this: 'LEFT-RIGHT-WOOF-WOOF, LEFT-RIGHT-WOOF-WOOF!' He would run up and down the column trying to catch us, but he never did.

We stayed in Harlow for a few weeks, and then at the end of October, we transferred to Newmarket. We were billeted in Dorothy Paget's Racing Stables. The stables had been cleared out for us, and we were issued with camp beds and palliasses. I can hear you saying not very comfortable, but I'm telling you, it was better than sleeping on the floor, which was made of cobble-stones. We were fitted out with new uniforms, including the fore-and-aft Glengarry hats, and for the first time we were issued with rifles. They were old Lee-Enfield 303s. No ammunition of course, but we still had our old eighteen-inch bayonets, so watch out Hitler!

After I was married I tried to get home as often as I could. Lily was staying with my Mum and Dad. Sometimes I hitch-hiked from Newmarket to Enfield.

It was fairly easy to pick up a lift, especially if you were in uniform. The regiment was under strength, so the numbers were made up by taking in new conscripts. We would march to Newmarket Station to meet them, with the regimental band leading the way. Most of the conscripts looked a sorry lot when they arrived – they were from all walks of life, all parts of the country, and they wore a fantastic variety of civvy gear. There were trilby hats, bowler hats, flat caps, I even saw one or two wearing plus-fours. None of them were particularly happy at being called up, and I knew it would be hard work training them. Nonetheless they turned out to be a great bunch of blokes, and many of them went on to become heroes.

6

I Become a Dad

We still had no guns, so we did a lot of square-bashing, and we gradually built up into a capable, well disciplined unit. One of the conscripts was a bloke called Albert Cardwell, and he and I became great mates. He came from St Helens in Lancashire, and he was a Rugby League player, so he was a pretty tough nut. He found it very difficult to cope with Army life, and was always in trouble. When we became buddies I managed to keep him on the straight and narrow, and before long he turned out to be a good soldier.

Lily had fallen pregnant not long after we were married. The time seemed to fly by, and all of a sudden I got a letter telling me the baby was due any time. I couldn't get home to be with Lily when our son was born, but I saw him soon after, and I'm telling you, I was as proud as a peacock. It seemed natural to call our son William after Lily's dad. She still hadn't got over losing him, and of course it pleased her dear mum. Billy was her first grandchild. He was also my mum and dad's first grandchild, so you can imagine how spoilt he was! Not only by his grandparents, but also by his doting uncles and aunties, all of whom were still living at home. My old Dad had a motor-bike and sidecar in those days, and now and again he would bring Lily and little Billy up to Newmarket to see me, and I would spend the day with them.

Because I happened to be the first in our unit to become a father, my mates had started to call me Pop. This was subsequently lengthened to Popeye, possibly influenced by the fact that I did a pretty fair imitation of Popeye the Sailorman.

It wasn't long before we started to train in earnest. We did unarmed combat, assault courses, shooting practice, and we were introduced to the Lewis gun. It was a light machine-gun, much favoured by the British Army, but it was a God-awful weapon. And of course, there was interminable drilling and square-bashing.

We did have some lighter moments, I was a member of the concert party, and if I say so myself, we were pretty good. We had some great performers, some had been conscripted directly from the musical profession. Our dance band was led by a trumpeter named Ted Hamer, who used to play with the Lou Praeger band. There was a saxophonist called Billy Shakespeare, and a terrific pianist, Freddy Michette. He could play anything! We had great fun putting the concerts together, and some of the sketches we put on were hilarious. I used to take part in the little plays and sketches, and now and then I had the opportunity to sing.

In May 1940 we were all devastated when we heard about the retreat to Dunkirk, our Army was nearly annihilated, but thank God, the British spirit saw us through. It was a miracle that so many of our boys were rescued and brought home. What courage! Not only them, but also those brave people who sailed across the Channel in their 'cockleshell' boats to do their bit for England.

We were certain that Hitler would take the opportunity to invade. If only he had known how unprepared we were he could have overrun us with no trouble at all. But of course, he didn't, thank goodness, and so we had another chance.

Ron with baby Bill, 1940. Courtesy of Mrs L. Davies.

7

Dunwich

We left Newmarket and went to a tiny little coastal village by the name of Dunwich in Suffolk. I suppose it must have made quite an impression on me because I've taken Lily and the boys on holiday there several times. I have taken great delight in pointing out to them exactly where we were camped along the clifftops, and where we carried out our various exercises.

Dunwich has a curious history; it was a busy port in Roman and medieval times. Unfortunately half of the town then fell into the sea. The local people say that at certain times of the year, if you listen very carefully, you can hear the old church bells ringing in the deep.

Anyway, we were supposed to be defending that stretch of coast, so we dug slit trenches along the clifftops and filled sand-bags. We slept in bell-tents, which were pitched just behind the trenches. There were fourteen men to a tent. If you've ever slept fourteen to a tent you will know what I mean when I tell you it was bloody uncomfortable! Talk about sardines in a tin! When you were on guard duty, or if you wanted to get up in the middle of the night, you couldn't help stepping on one or two faces. However, we managed. In fact we had a few laughs.

We were very short of weapons, and as I mentioned earlier, we wouldn't have stood a chance of stopping an invasion. There were two of us to a trench, and I was teamed up with a bloke called Frank Farndell, or to give him his proper name, Flossie!

He had a Lewis gun and one magazine, and I had a Boys anti-tank .55 rifle, and ten rounds of ammo. The Boyes had one hell of a kick, but it wouldn't have made a hole in a cardboard box, let alone knock a tank out. We also had a twelve-inch searchlight, operated by a Lister engine. We tried it out, and it gave a reasonable light. One night when Flossie and I were on watch, he turned to me and said, 'You do realise Pop don't you, if Jerry was to come the first thing he would do would be to shoot this bleedin' light out!' I remember saying with great feeling, 'Sod this for a game of soldiers, I want to go home!'

Our one consolation was the knowledge that the British Navy was out there somewhere. There were a few scares, and we were stood to several times. On one occasion we were attacked by a German ME 109. He flew so low along the beach that we were actually looking down on him. We loosed a few shots off, but to no avail. We were ticked off for wasting ammo.

We had troops all along that part of the Suffolk coast, and now and then we got time off to go to Southend where another section of our Regiment were manning a twenty-five pounder. It was situated at the end of the pier, and we gave it a good look over because this was going to be our main weapon in the near future.

On one occasion we were taken to an Army Depot just outside of Lowestoft to try out our gas-masks and gas-capes. We went into a chamber with the masks and capes on, and then we were told to take them off so that we could recognise the smell of poison gas. One whiff, and then we quickly put the masks back on. It was evil! After a while we went back out into the fresh air, and most of us were as sick as dogs.

Then we had to bare our arms, and a little drop of mustard gas was placed directly onto our skin. Almost immediately a painful blister erupted, treated straight away of course by the medic on hand. We all hoped fervently that the Germans wouldn't use it!

Anyone who has ever been to Dunwich will know what a delightful little place it is. I often felt it was a shame that it had to be desecrated by all the Army equipment that littered the place. There were miles and miles of barbed wire, and piles of sand-bags. It certainly made that beautiful place look ugly.

After the invasion scare faded away we moved away from Dunwich, and went to a place just outside of Beccles, just a few miles further north. We took over a big old house called Redisham Hall. It was part of a huge estate, and belonged to our Brigadier, Sir Ronald Phayre. Ordinary ranks were under canvas in the grounds, while the house was used as Headquarters and for the officers' billets.

All our officers seemed to be aristocrats. It was Sir So-and-So, and Lord Something or the Other. Our Colonel, J.F. Todhunter, was at one time Lord Lieutenant of Essex. Then there was Captain the Honourable Chris Sidgewick, and Captain Philo Vance, who was a famous steeplechase jockey. You'd have thought they would be a toffee-nosed lot, but they weren't, they were a good bunch of blokes. They had their own horses brought in, and some of them joined in with the local hunt. The grounds were teeming with pheasants, so nearly every week there was a shoot, and more often than not we would be paid a shilling a day to act as beaters.

Major R. Gosling took over 431 Battery in Autumn 1941, and Regimental Sergeant Major Hector Bennett took up his duties at the same time.

413 Battery Group photograph pre-1944. Ron is in the top row, third from left. Courtesy of Mrs L. Davies.

8

Trigger and Me

Talking about pheasants, it's about time I introduced you to one of the most colourful characters I ever met. Trigger's real name was George Bentley, and he got his nick-name because he was a dead shot. He was a fantastic bloke, I've never known anyone like him. It was a privilege to be his mate, and although I only knew him for a few short months, I still have these vivid memories of him.

I'm not very tall, about five foot eight, and Trigger was shorter than me. Nevertheless, what he lacked in height he made up for in build. He had the shoulders and arms of a heavyweight wrestler, and was immensely strong. There were a number of stunts he used to perform to show off his strength and toughness. For instance, he would get one of us to throw a cricket ball as high in the air as we could, and then he would head it like a football. He had long hair, and he would challenge two or three blokes to grab it and try to pull him over. Nobody ever could. Sometimes he would get us to hold his hair as tightly as we could, and then he would climb onto a table and let us dangle. I've seen him with two hefty soldiers dangling, holding them off the ground with just his hair.

Some of the things he did made me wince. Like taking a half round file, and filing his teeth! For all that, he was a big-hearted, amiable sort of chap, I never knew him to get into a fight.

We got up to a few escapades, Trigger and me. It's a wonder we didn't get into trouble. One day he came to me quite excited, and told me he had found an entrance to the wine-cellar of the big house. It was a double trap door set into the ground, similar to the trap door of a pub. It was round the side of the house, and was fairly well hidden. Most of our mates liked a drink, so we decided to give the blokes in our tent a treat. Late one evening we set off with a torch, and a length of rope. Trigger had taught me how to move without making a noise or attracting attention, so we got to the trap door with no trouble.

We soon had the door open, and I lowered Trigger down on the rope. After a few moments the rope went slack, and then I felt a tug on it, and up came a case of wine. I untied it, let the rope down again, and Trigger climbed out. I kept an eye out while Trigger silently fastened the door, and we scooted off back to our tent. Boy, were we popular that night! I don't remember what label was on the bottles, only that the wine was red, fruity, and delicious! There were eight bottles in that case, and it all went that night. We had a great booze-up, but we didn't attempt it again. Even though Trigger had told me of the enormous quantity and variety of wine in that cellar, we decided that it was just too risky!

Trigger was a typical country boy, and poaching was second nature to him. He didn't see anything immoral in it. He took great delight in teaching city boys like me the ways of the countryside, and that included snaffling a pheasant or two.

After church parade one Sunday, Trigger and I went for a walk in the woods. He was scouring the ground, obviously searching for something, and I was curious to see him take some chalk from his pocket, and mark off certain trees. I asked him what he was doing, and he explained that he had looked for pheasant droppings under the trees, as this would indicate where they roosted at night.

Later that day, as it started to get dark, we went off again. I was carrying a torch, and Trigger had a steel catapult and some lead shot. When we came to the first tree he had marked, he told me to shine the torch up into the branches. There was a big fat pheasant, sitting right at the top. It sat quite still, mesmerised by the light. I told you what a crack shot Trigger was with a rifle, but believe me, he was even deadlier with a catapult. He loaded it with a lead pellet, took aim, and down came the poor bird, dead as a doornail. We got two more birds that evening, he stuffed them up his blouse, and I stuffed the other one up mine.

We set off furtively back to our tent, but to our dismay, who should we bump into but Regimental Sergeant Major Hector Bennett! He looked us up and down, and said, 'Good evening lads.' We replied as one, 'Good evening sir!' He fixed Trigger with his beady eye, and then he asked in a stern voice, 'Bentley, what have you got under your tunic?' 'Nothing, Sergeant Major' was the innocent reply. 'Then what's that long thing hanging down between your legs!' roared Hector. I looked, and there, poking out from under Trigger's blouse, was the long tail feather of a pheasant. Boy, did we think we were in trouble! However, the luck of the Daviesses prevailed, and with a twinkle in his eye, old Hector let us off, provided we gave him one of the birds.

Trigger knew how to hang the pheasants for a few days until they were ready for eating, and we got our cooks to prepare them for us. What a feast we had. Pheasant must have gone down well in the sergeants' mess too, because a few days later, the RSM came to see us, and asked us to get a few more.

I learned so much just from being with Trigger. I've mentioned how he taught me to move through woods and underbrush without making a noise, he also told me how to approach game from upwind, and many other aspects of woodcraft. He knew the names of all the birds and woodland creatures, all the different types of trees, what grew there that could be eaten – including the difference between mushrooms and toadstools! Much of what he taught me stood me in good stead when I finally went into combat.

Poor old Trigger didn't survive the war. In fact, he didn't even make it to D-Day. I've told you he was a typical country boy, he didn't believe in doctors. He would use the old country remedies if he was ill. He developed an abscess on the back of his neck, so he did no more than slice the top off with a razor-blade to drain it, and tied the wound up with a handkerchief. The razor-blade must have been rusty, because septicaemia set in, and after a short illness, he died.

We were all stunned, it was so sudden. Old Trigger was such a vital, lively character. His funeral took place at his home town of Sudbury, and a squad of us went along to give him a military funeral. I really missed Trigger. It would have been great to have him beside me when we went into action. I still miss him.

Senior NCOs of the Essex Yeomanry. Hector Bennett is in the middle of the seated row. Courtesy of the Essex Yeomanry.

9

I Get a Stripe

I don't want you to think that army life was just one lark after another, we worked damned hard. There were daily route marches, regular keep-fit drills, and we were constantly training in unarmed combat. We were all required to go to the firing range two or three times a week, and I did pretty well. Not as good as dear old Trigger, but I soon qualified for my marksman's badge, which earned me an extra threepence a day! It also resulted in me getting my first stripe, so now I was Lance Bombardier Davies.

During our stay at Redisham Hall, some of us were taken down to King's Cross Station in London to mount a guard. Saboteurs and the IRA were causing a lot of trouble in London and the railway stations were prime targets. You wouldn't believe the maze of tunnels there are under King's Cross. We had to patrol down there, and it was filthy! Years and years of soot had accumulated from generations of old steam locomotives. We were issued with civilian overcoats to keep our uniforms clean. Another of our duties was to mount a ceremonial guard on one of the platforms. This always attracted a big audience, so the NCOs were very hot on the bullshit. Loads of blanco and Duraglit!

We did twenty-four hours on and twenty-four off, so when I was off duty I was able to go home for the day via Liverpool Street, which was great. Lily had managed to get a council house in Redlands Road near Brimsdown, and I really felt proud that going home on leave was to our home, mine and Lily's.

That was a nice little interlude, but it couldn't last and after a month we went back to Redisham Hall. After a short while we were on the move again, this time to a place called Brome Hall in Norfolk. Brome Hall was another big country house set in several acres of land. As at Redisham Hall the 'Other Ranks' were under canvas in the grounds, and the house was Regimental H.Q.

We had been there for a week or so, when we were informed that some of us could have our families to come and live with us. I wrote Lily a letter, and she came up to Norfolk with our son. We shared an old cottage with another couple.

Battery 431 officers, Scarborough, 1942. Top Row: Frank Macaskie, unknown, unknown, T. Richardson, Eric Edwards, X. Davenport, Richard Foreman. Second Row: Ken Munro, Max Beale, Dick Gosling, Clive Sidgewich. Courtesy of General Richardson.

Talk about primitive! There was no electricity, and our only light was provided by hurricane lamps and candles. The toilet was an earth closet! The owners of the cottage were still living there, so there were six adults, plus our kids. We were very cramped for space. Still, it was lovely having Lily and little Billy staying with me and away from that horrible bombing London was getting.

I remember that while we were at Brome Hall the officers organised a Regimental dance. As I've said before, our officers were all decent blokes, but there was still a lot of class distinction in the Army. A poster was put up advertising the dance, and it read like this:

The Colonel cordially invites the officers and their ladies, the N.C.O.s' and their wives, and the other ranks and their women, to a dance.

What snobbery there was then!

I couldn't go anyway because I was on guard duty, but Lily went with one of the other wives, and they had a good time. We didn't seem to stay very long in any one place, and after six weeks at Brome, we were on the move again. We went to a place called Thelveston, which wasn't all that far away. We arranged for Lily to stay at a nice little cottage there, but after only a week, we moved again! This time we were in Sheringham, Norfolk.

It was as a result of this move that I had my first little spat with Lily. I really blotted my copy-book! I was due for a week's leave, so we arranged that when I arrived at Sheringham I would catch a train to Norwich, change there and catch another train to Diss, and then go to meet Lily at Thelveston so that we could travel home together. That was the plan, but unfortunately I boobed. I got on the wrong train, and it didn't stop. It went straight through to Liverpool Street. I felt such a berk, but there was nothing I could do.

I went home to Redlands Road, and sent Lily a telegram, telling her that I would meet her at Liverpool Street the next day. The lady who owned the cottage told her that she shouldn't travel because Billy had the measles, nevertheless Lily got a taxi to Diss and caught the train to Liverpool Street. I met her there with her brother Harry who was on leave from the Navy. We couldn't get onto the platform to help her, so the poor girl had to struggle along with Billy in her arms wrapped in a blanket, and carrying all the luggage. She didn't speak to me for a week, and as Harry said at the time, who could blame her?

When I got back to Sheringham I found that we were billeted in a big hotel called The Metropole. We slept six to a room, but we didn't mind, because it was a vast improvement on sleeping under canvas. There was a Lewis gun on the roof, and we got to use it several times when there were air-raids. Not that we ever hit anything. We also went out to assist the fire brigade with some of the burning buildings.

It was at Sheringham that I had my first experience of driving a tracked vehicle. Nothing like driving a conventional motor, believe you me! It was a Bren gun carrier, and we went out in a convoy, taking turns at driving. When it came to my turn, we had got a bit behind the others, so I put my foot down to try to catch them up. They must have turned off without me seeing them because the next thing I saw was a policeman who was frantically signalling for us to turn right. Trouble was, I was going too fast. I turned the wheel hard, and we spun round and round the poor old copper. Needless to say, I didn't get to drive again that day.

One of our duties was to mount a fire-picket, which involved patrolling the hotel to make sure that the blackout procedures were properly carried out. The

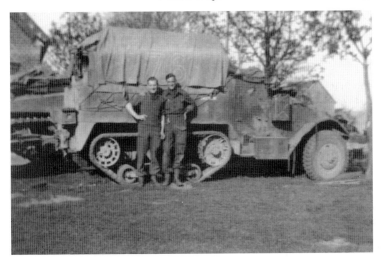

A tracked transport vehicle with D Troop. Courtesy of Frank Holt.

patrol consisted of four men and an NCO. One night when I was in charge some stupid berks who had been out on a late pass left a toilet light on all night. We had carried out our duties to the letter and had been allowed to go to bed after lights-out, but these idiots got back after that.

In the morning I was ordered to report to the CO, because the police had complained. As I had been in charge, I was held responsible and duly went before a lady magistrate. She said that there had been a lot of trouble from the military, and was going to make an example of me. I wanted to defend myself, and explain the situation, but the CO had ordered me to plead guilty. He said he didn't want to upset the local authorities. I was fined two pounds and ten shillings, plus two and six costs. The Army paid the fine, but stopped it out of my wages at two bob a week. My mates had a whip round, so I wasn't out of pocket. Which was just as well, because my pay was only ten shillings and sixpence a week! It was nice of the blokes, but of course, we were all comrades, and that was the sort of thing we did for one another. My Dad was livid when he heard about it. He wrote to the *Daily Mirror*, but nothing ever came of it.

10

Training in Earnest

News came much to our delight that we were going to be equipped with the new twenty-five pounder gun. We were ordered to go to Larkshill Barracks on Salisbury Plain to take delivery. We took charge of over sixteen guns, plus gun carriages called Limbers, and Quads. The Quads were four-wheeled three-ton trucks, which looked like tanks except that they had wheels instead of tracks. There was room inside for all our personal gear, and seats for all the crew. The crew was made up as follows: number one, usually a sergeant, number two, this was the gun layer, numbers three and four were the loaders, and number five was the driver. The limbers carried all the ammunition: high explosive shells, armour-piercing shells, and a variety of others. There is no doubt that the twenty-five pounder was the best artillery piece used during the war. It had a rifled barrel, which caused the shell to rotate clockwise. This gave it a range of three miles and extreme accuracy. The only weapon to come anywhere near it was the German eighty-eight millimetre.

I trained as a gun layer, which was quite a complicated job. I passed my course, and got my gun layer's badge, which meant that I got a further three pence a day. It was very hard work operating one of these weapons, but we had a good crew, and soon made easy work of it. We all had to learn to drive the Quad and it was great fun driving it around Salisbury Plain. We trained for several months in this location, and we took part in competitions with other Regiments. The object was to get your gun into position and be first to hit the target. We won a couple of times, and our Commanding Officer was delighted, because it meant that we were now fully operational. I was even more delighted, because I was awarded my second stripe!

Our crew consisted of Sergeant Bill Wilby who came from Walthamstow, myself as number two, Crow Bannock, also from Walthamstow, and Ralph Diamond from Manchester as numbers three and four, and Flash Gorman as number five. Bill later made something of a name for himself over an incident at

Flamborough Head in Yorkshire. Some time in 1942 it was. Practice firing was taking place on the range there, and Bill fired his gun while the Engineers were still fiddling about making adjustments to the targets. Crow got his nickname from his weird habit of sleeping with his eyes wide open. Very strange. Used to give me the willies. Sorry to digress.

We moved to a camp at Warminster, and we would go out for days on end doing exercises which were referred to as schemes. Salisbury Plain must have been covered with the marks of our tracks. While we were at Warminster I went on several courses, the first of which was a voice training course. This was held at Bulford Barracks, which had a huge parade ground. The course involved what was known as a 'Dumb Squad'. This was a group of squaddies who would obey any order you gave them, right or wrong. So, we had to drill this 'Dumb Squad' and the instructor would let them get as far away as possible, almost out of sight, and then he would say, "Right, bring them back!" You then had to bellow at the top of your voice, "About turn!" Still, I thoroughly enjoyed it, it taught me to project my voice, which stood me in good stead when I took up band work and amateur operatics after the war.

The next course I did was on small arms, and I learned all there is to know about the Bren gun and the PIAT gun. The Bren was a formidable weapon, it was classified as a light machine gun, and was incredibly accurate. If you fired it in a fixed position and fired, say, ten rounds, the bullets would all go through the same hole in the target. We had to be able to strip and reassemble it blindfold, and we held competitions to see who was the fastest. The record was ninety seconds. I became very adept at this task, and I believe that I could still do it. (Not in ninety seconds though!)

The PIAT was a completely different kettle of fish. The word PIAT was an acronym, it stood for Projectile Infantry Anti Tank. It was spring-loaded, and to cock it you had to sit on the ground and hold the weapon between your legs and put your feet into what looked like stirrups. Then you had to pull the spring back. It took a lot of strength, believe me! The bomb that it fired was as big as a large turnip with a long narrow point about eight inches long. The idea was that the point pierced the armour of a tank and when the bomb went off the blast would knock out the occupants. As history will show, it worked. But it was a swine of a weapon to fire, it had one hell of a kick. In fact the bloke who invented it broke his back while he was testing it.

Not only did we have to learn about the weapons, we also had to learn to be instructors, and how to conduct a lecture. Our instructor would call you out, give you an object, and you would have a minute to talk about it. When it came to my turn, he gave me a piece of string. What can you say about a piece of string? Not a lot, but being blessed with the gift of the gab, I managed. And so I became a Regimental Small Arms Instructor. This earned me yet another three pence a day. I was getting rich!

I went on a camouflage course, and having camouflaged a gun site, we were taken up in a plane a few at a time to see if we could spot it from the air. The plane was a Westland Lysander, and there was only room for four in the seats provided. So, guess who the unlucky bloke was who had to lie in the observer's blip which was underneath the pilot's seat? It was my first ever flight, and I needed a clean pair of pants by the time we landed! And even after all the trouble we had taken, we spotted our gun site with no trouble at all.

We often used to moan about all this training because we couldn't see the purpose of it all, but of course, in the event, it made all the difference. I still believe that the British Army is second to none when it comes to training.

Although we were fully operational, we were still under strength, so a number of soldiers were transferred from our sister Regiment, the 146th. They were an Armoured Car Regiment operating in the Far East, and they had been almost wiped out. We became part of the 30th Corps under the command of General Brian Horrocks. 30th Corps was part of the British 2nd Army, commanded by General Miles Dempsey who later designated us as an Armoured Unit.

The 2nd Army Headquarters were in Yorkshire, so we set off from Salisbury Plain in a huge convoy. We made for Nottingham, where we stopped for the night, and the next day we reached Thirsk in Yorkshire. We were billeted on Thirsk race course, and our section was under the Totalisator – we were what you might call a sure bet!

One day we were invited to have a ride, there were plenty of horses available, and I chose this docile nag and walked him around the course at a very slow pace. Some of the other lads were really good riders, particularly a bloke called Ginger Wiltshire who had been a huntsman in Civvy Street. He was galloping his horse around the course as if he were in a race. As he went past me he must have brushed against my horse, because all of a sudden my quiet little nag took off like Red Rum. He jumped the white rails, and I went straight over his head. I managed to hang on to him, and some of the riders gathered round, urging me to remount and jump him back over the rails. I graciously declined, and walked him back to the stables. That was the end of my riding ambitions!

We spent a week at Thirsk and then moved on to an army camp at Pickering, right on the edge of the Yorkshire Dales. Once again we started our training, and went out on the Dales on schemes. We spent many a cold night in that lovely part of the country. It was now November 1941, and I received a telegram one day telling me that I was now the proud father of another son, little Stephen. I managed to get a week's leave, and went home. I arrived at King's Cross late that night, and found myself right in the middle of a terrifying air-raid. I thought to myself, 'blimey, our folks at home are having a much worse time than we are. And we're supposed to be defending them!' The only bus I could get terminated at Tramway Avenue Edmonton, so I had to walk the last three miles. I arrived home in the early hours of the morning, and rather than wake Lily up, I sat on the doorstep for hours. I had a smashing week's leave with my lovely wife, and enjoyed being Daddy to baby Stephen and little Billy, who was now eighteen months old.

11

Who was Dick Smith?

On my return from leave I was sent to Catterick on yet another course. I thought that Catterick was a God-awful place, probably made worse by the fact that winter was setting in. I was on an intensive training course on assault and survival. This included the usual assault course, cross-country running, and physical exercises. One day we were taken out in pairs in a sealed lorry, and dropped off miles away from anywhere. A compass was our sole aid in finding our way back to camp.

My mate and I found our way to a road, and as luck would have it, a local farmer gave us a lift all the way back. We didn't want to be too early, so we found a pub and stayed there for the day. We had a meal, and played darts to pass the time, and went back to camp as it was getting dark. To our amazement we were first back! Some of the other poor souls were out all night.

After that I went to Barnard Castle and spent a fortnight on the firing range. We got back to Pickering just as the bad weather really started. It was the worst winter for years. Heavy snow blocked all the local roads, in some places it was eight feet deep. The main road to Scarborough was completely blocked, so we were called in. It took a long time to clear it, I remember a place called Sutton Bank, the snow was really deep there. It was a week before traffic was able to get through, and I have never been so cold in all my life.

Well, it was already 1942, and we had still not been sent into action. We were beginning to think that the war would be over before we could put all that training to good use. We were fit, fighting fit, and in our opinion we were more than ready to take on the might of the German Army. So what did they do? They sent us up to Northumberland on more schemes. We were there for a month, in a place named Otterburn. It was right up on the Scottish border, very desolate.

I remember a nice old country pub there where we used to go in the evenings. It was called The First and Last. The first time we went there, we saw a

Ron wearing a greatcoat in the snow. Courtesy of
Mrs L. Davies.

group of old boys sitting around playing cards. We asked if we could have a drink,
and they told us to just help ourselves. Oh yes, we were made very welcome.

I played for the regimental football team, and the cricket team. We also played
hockey, and I even had a go at rugby, but that didn't last for long. We did a lot
of cross-country running, keeping up our level of fitness. I'd love to be that fit
now!

Some time in late 1942 the 191st Field Regiment was formed, and as part of
the shake-up I was transferred from 431 Battery to 413 Battery. My new CO was
Captain Sidgewick, he was a good officer and a real gentleman.

There was one amusing incident at Otterburn that I must tell you about. We had
to mount a ceremonial guard, and the changing of the guard took place at six pm
every evening. As I was now a Bombardier (Corporal) I had to take my turn as
Guard Commander. Earlier on that day someone found out that the orderly officer
who was taking the guard mounting that evening was Lieutenant William Strong,
who was without doubt a bit of a twit. So, the lads dared me to play a joke on
him. The last order that the new Guard Commander gives is 'New Guard, to the
Guard-Room, dismiss!' But instead of 'dismiss' they dared me to say 'Dick Smith!'
The guard mounting went well, and when it came time for me to dismiss my men,
I shouted, 'New Guard, to the Guard-Room, Dick Smith!' I turned to the officer,

413 Battery Group photo pre-1944. Ron is in the third row from the top, fifth from the right. Courtesy of Mrs L. Davies.

threw him up a salute, and he said, 'Well done Bombardier, a good turn-out!' Later on that evening RSM Hector Bennett came to the Guard-Room for his usual cup of tea, and he said to me, 'That was a good guard mounting, Bombardier, but who the hell is this bloke Dick Smith?' Luckily for me old Hector had a sense of humour, and he walked off chuckling to himself.

We went back to Pickering, and shortly after we were on the move again, this time to Wales. We were in a camp just outside of Towyn. Now, there is a humourous story relating to my exploits in Towyn, but it is probably inappropriate to print it here. If you want to know the details, you'll have to ask my sister Betty. The beach at Towyn is very long, we used to play football on the nice firm sand. It was a very pretty area, and we did a lot of training on the Brecon Heights. After we had been there for a while we were told that we were losing our guns, and were to be issued with Self-Propelled Guns, referred to as SPs. In other words we were getting tanks.

A Sexton SP gun with D Troop. Courtesy of Frank Holt.

There were three types of SP, two made in the USA, and one made in Canada. They were all built on a Sherman tank chassis, but the American versions had 105mm guns, as opposed to the Canadian version which was equipped with our favourite gun, the twenty-five pounder. It was called a Sexton [see Notes on the Text].

We moved down to Ilfracombe in Dorset to hand over our guns, Limbers and Quads with a full ceremonial parade. So there we were, a regiment of gunners without guns. Still, we had a good time in Ilfracombe. We went along the coast to Lynmouth, and did some abseiling on the cliffs there. There was an open-air swimming pool at Lynmouth, we spent a great deal of time relaxing there, but it all went a bit sour when one of our blokes was drowned while having a swim. It was all a bit of a mystery, and we never did find out what really happened. [See Notes on the Text.]

12

First Contact with the Yanks

We moved to Frome in Somerset on 15 March 1943, and I was ordered to go with some of the other NCOs to an American army camp near Bournemouth to learn about these SPs. We set off in a three-ton truck and found our way to the American base. We drove up to the main gate, and Major Dick Gosling got out and approached the scruffy looking American sentry. This individual was leaning against the gate and smoking a fat cigar. He said to our Major, 'Hi bub, what can I do for you?' If one of us had acted like that we would have been sent to the Glasshouse for life!

We reported to the office and were shown to our quarters, and then went to the mess hall for a meal. After we had eaten we realised that the Yanks were being looked after a damn sight better than we were. Their food was better, they got better pay, their uniforms were smarter, but their discipline was lousy! Having said that they looked after us very well. We were each assigned to an American tank crew, but to be honest I learned more about poker than I did about SPs. I could only stand by and watch them play, I could never afford the kind of stakes they were playing for. Gambling is legal in the American army and they had a properly organised casino where even the officers joined in. The most popular game was craps, and you should have seen the amount of money that changed hands.

The British had the NAAFI, and the Yanks had their own equivalent, the United Services Organisation. The difference was we had to pay for tea and wads, they didn't! Anyway while we were there we stocked up on doughnuts and coffee. We left the Yanks to their poker and craps, and made our way back to Frome, and after a week the NCOs were on their way to Brandon in Suffolk to pick up our new SPs. We travelled by train and spent the night at a Royal Ordnance depot when we got there. The next day we had a look at our new toys, and before I go any further I had better explain all the ins and outs of an SP.

The Sexton Self-Propelled Gun was built on a Sherman tank body and weighed 39 tons. It was powered by a 350 horsepower, Wrights Whirlwind radial aero engine, and it was air-cooled. The armament was a twenty-five pounder field gun, mounted left of centre in an open-top superstructure. Elevation was forty degrees, and it had a traverse of fifteen degrees right, and twenty-five degrees left. There was also a .50 inch Browning heavy machine gun mounted at the front of the hull. Two Browning .303 machine guns were mounted on either side of the driver's compartment, and there were various other types of small arms including grenade launchers.

The engine used 100 octane aviation spirit. The fuel was kept in four tanks, two vertical tanks holding 25 gallons each and two horizontal tanks holding 50 gallons each. An extra 60 gallons were kept in Jerry cans on the back.

The standard stock of ammunition carried was 12 armour-piercing shells, 1,000 rounds of .303 cartridges, 100 high explosive shells and 2,000 rounds of .50 cartridges. There was also a box of grenades, a box of flares, and 20 smoke canisters. The twenty-five pounder had the usual gun loading equipment, but in addition it had an open sight, which was like a telescopic sight on a rifle. This was used for short-range shooting. What with all that fuel and the ammo, it was like a travelling time bomb!

It was fitted with rubber tracks for use in this country, so that it didn't churn up the roads too much, but these would be changed for steel when we got into action. There were five forward gears, four ordinary gears plus a booster gear, and reverse gear. Starting up was quite a procedure, first of all you had to prime the cylinders with neat fuel. Then you had to press the starter and the booster starter at the same time. When it did start it belched flames out of the exhaust, so there had to be a man standing at the back with a fire extinguisher just in case. If there was snow around as there frequently was when we were training, or in action, it would melt it for yards around. SPs were pigs to drive, you have to remember that there was no steering wheel. You steered with two tillers, which also acted as brakes. If you drove on a road that had a camber, you were continually pulling on the right hand tiller to keep straight. The driving position was pretty awful, I remember that you had to physically lift your foot onto the clutch. Top speed was 28mph on a road, but cross-country it would only do 18mph. Another incredible statistic was that it only did three quarters of a mile to the gallon. Not much good for popping down the shops!

After spending the night at the depot in Brandon we went to the local railway yard, and saw that our SPs had been loaded onto flat railway trucks. The crews had been allocated to Pullman carriages. We set off for Liverpool Street in London, and it dawned on me that we would be going through Brimsdown Station, just about a mile from our house. I scribbled out a short note to Lily and wrapped it around a bar of chocolate. The idea was that I would throw it out of the window as we went through Brimsdown. We got nearer and nearer; we went through Broxbourne, Cheshunt and Waltham Cross, and then as we went through Enfield Lock we started to slow down, and as we were going past Albany Park, the train stopped. There we were, just a few hundred yards from my home and family, and I couldn't do a thing about it. We were there for a good ten minutes and there were me and the lads standing at the window shouting 'Oi, Lil, Mrs Davies!' We started to move very slowly, so slowly in fact that I was able to give my note to a porter at Brimsdown, and I asked him to deliver it for me and he did!

Well after a lot of shunting around, we finally made it back to Frome. We unloaded our SPs and parked them in the town park, which had been commandeered for the purpose. We spent the next few weeks becoming thoroughly familiar with our new weapons. We also took delivery of a couple of Sherman tanks which were to be used as our forward observers. We had been divided into Troops, we were in C for 'Charlie' Troop, and our SP was named 'Coggeshall'. After that we started intensive training. It was completely different to our previous training, but we soon got to grips with it. We had great fun shooting at derelict vehicles with the cannon, and practised on the Browning by firing at a drogue towed by a light aircraft. The guns were very effective at both short and long range, and before long we were once more fully operational and ready for action.

We were driving to Salisbury Plain every day for training, and our CO ordered us to stop on the way back every day to clean our vehicles. This was so we didn't leave a trail of mud through the streets of Frome. The local residents were very grateful for that!

I have referred here and there in this history, to the Glasshouse, which is army slang for military prison. There have been lots of jokes about the Glasshouse, but let me tell you, they were awful places. It was while I was at Frome that I got as near as I ever want to get to one. One of my mates and I had to escort a bloke to military prison at Allerton in Yorkshire. We went to London by train, and then caught a train to York. We were picked up at the station by a truck which took us to Allerton. I can't remember the poor bloke's name, but I can still see his face. All he had been convicted of was overstaying his leave by four days. The truck dropped us off at the gate with all his gear and this big Redcap came striding over. He seemed gigantic to me, full of menace; the peak of his cap was jammed so low on his head that you couldn't see his eyes. He shouted 'Pick up your kit!' I automatically bent down to help the prisoner pick it up, and the Redcap was furious. 'Not you! Him!' he screamed. So the poor little sod had to pick up the lot. The Redcap then shouted out 'At the double!' So the three of us had to run across the parade ground, him dropping bits all the way and stopping to retrieve them, until we got to the office and signed him over. What a relief it was to get out of there. I did feel sorry for the poor chap.

13

North of the Border

We had no idea at that time what we were actually being trained for. There were all sorts of rumours going about, but nothing definite. There was talk of a second front, but where? And when? And what was going to be our part in it? We were convinced that we were ready for anything and were raring to go. So we thought. In actual fact the training that was to come made what we had done in the past look like a picnic.

There was a nice little hall in the camp where we used to put on concerts, and one day Captain Sidgewick told me that he wanted me to take charge of a squad to get the hall ready for an ENSA concert. I had had the chance of joining ENSA but like a stupid bugger I turned the offer down. I thought that my mates would think that I was trying to get out of fighting. I didn't want them to think that I was a coward. What a twit! I've often regretted throwing away that opportunity. So many professional actors and entertainers got their start through ENSA, and I think I might have had the talent to give it a try. Ah well!

Anyway, we started to set up this hall ready for the concert, when in walked this bloke. He was dressed in the ENSA uniform, but he was only a private. He came across to me and said 'Are you in charge here?' I told him that I was, and he started giving me orders. 'I want this here, and that there', he said. So, I got on my high horse didn't I? I pointed to my two stripes and I said, 'Oi mate, what do you think these are, banana skins?' It turned out his name was Charlie Chester!

Christmas came and went, and we were on the move once more, this time all the way up to Scotland. We set off in a huge convoy of tank transporters, and on the first day we made it to Doncaster. We spent the night on Doncaster race course.

Next day we set out again and got as far as Kilmarnock. From there we travelled to Greenock on the Clyde. Our SPs were loaded onto LCTs (Landing Craft, Tanks) and we were all ferried across to Rothesay on the Isle of Bute. We left the SPs on board and went to a camp just outside of Rothesay. We thought that the big day had come and that we were going into action. In fact the real invasion training was only just about to start. We had quite a bit of leisure time and were able to have a look around that lovely town. I met an old seaman who told me that Bute was part of a group of islands called the Kyles of Bute, which were in the Gulf Stream. The sea around them was a beautiful navy blue colour, I never tired of looking at the wonderful view. The tourists paid a fortune to cruise around these islands, and we were getting it for free!

We unloaded our SPs and parked them in a huge car park. Our CO wanted us to get the feeling of being at sea, because we were going to be spending a lot of time on it. So we went aboard one of the LCTs and went on a tour of the islands. Because the LCT had no keel it didn't cut through the waves like an ordinary boat, so there was a lot of pitching and tossing. We were taken to one island, and the boat grounded just short of the beach. We started to take our boots and socks off to wade ashore, but our Brigade Sergeant Major Jacksie Brown pushed his way to the front, determined to lead the way. He waved his swagger stick and shouted 'Charge!' and leaped off of the ramp. Amidst great hilarity he promptly disappeared under the water! The LCT had grounded on

Scene on board LCT, 1944. Courtesy of the Essex Yeomanry.

a shelf and poor old Jacksie had jumped into water eight feet deep. You should have heard the language when we pulled him out! I don't think he ever lived it down. We had to find another place to land, and we all jumped about in the water like a bunch of kids at the seaside.

All this was great fun, but then our training started in earnest. Our first job was to waterproof the SPs. We did this by plugging every nook and cranny we could find with a material called Bostick which looked something like plasticine but set as hard as metal after a few hours. The exhaust and air-intake were raised, which meant that theoretically the SP could drive in six feet of water. Unfortunately it didn't work out in practice as you will see! We started landing practice, and were relieved to find that our waterproofing had worked. The training went on for months and we became pretty good at landing the SPs in up to four feet of water. In the middle of the summer we were told to pick up our gear, because we were on the move once again. The LCTs took us back to Greenock, where the SPs were loaded onto transporters. After a long journey we reached a little town called Muir of Ord which is just north of Inverness. The

Scene on board LCT, 1944. Courtesy of the Essex Yeomanry.

army camp there was made up of mostly Nissen huts, and we made ourselves very comfortable.

The surrounding countryside where we were training was very mountainous, and we often came across crystal-clear streams and waterfalls. I recall one day when the sun was beating down, and we were all sweating buckets after a particularly strenuous session. Nearby was this lovely stream which came cascading down from the mountains. It was clear and inviting, about six feet deep. We stripped off all our gear and dived in. The breath immediately left my body, and my skin felt as if it was on fire. I have never, ever experienced water as cold before or since. A bit naive I suppose, when you consider that the streams were created from melting snow. Mind you, it did cool us down.

One day six of the crews including us were taken down to Inverness and taken on board an LCT. At first glance it appeared to be loaded with tanks, but on closer inspection we found out that they were dummies made out of plywood. We were told that we would be sailing the next morning, but we weren't told where to. This all seemed a bit strange, but it didn't bother us, we just shrugged our shoulders and followed orders.

That evening we played cards with some of the crew in the wardroom. There was a high swell in the harbour and the boat was rocking about a fair bit. One of our lads, a chap called Freddie Joyce, had to keep on getting up and going out on deck to be sick. Us rotten lot took the mickey out of him without mercy, and after a while he had to give up and went off to bed. The rest of us carried on playing for a while and eventually we packed up too. I went up on deck to fill the ocean up with a little more water, and as I was doing so the boat gave a sudden lurch and I was as sick as a dog! Served me right for mocking the afflicted!

The next morning we sailed out into the North Sea and were out there all day. It was very odd, there was a whole fleet which appeared to be just sailing up and down to no apparent purpose. I asked one of the naval officers what was going on. He told me that the Navy were doing a dummy run to confuse the enemy. It may or may not have confused the Germans, it certainly confused the hell out of me! We returned to Muir of Ord the next day.

There was one incident at Muir of Ord that makes me chuckle now, although it didn't seem all that funny at the time. We had a combustion stove in the centre of our hut, and it usually fell to the newer recruits to light it each morning. On this particular day, two bright young sparks decided that the fire would burn up more quickly if they used sticks of cordite to light it with. Sticks of cordite look something like spaghetti, and when you light them they burn and splutter like sparklers. What these two idiots didn't realise was that if cordite is packed into a confined space and lit, it will explode.

Anyway, they put the cordite into the stove along with some wood and coal, shut the door of the stove, and then laid a trail of cordite along the floor and out of the hut door. Then they lit the fuse and ran off.

I was having a wash and shave at the time. All I heard was this enormous bang, I thought at first that we were having an air raid. We all rushed into the hut, and you should have seen the mess! The stove was in pieces, and the blast had gone up the chimney and down the side of the hut, burning off all of the paint. The room was filled with smoke and the wall and floors were festooned with shirts, tunics, bits of webbing, blankets etc. Some of the beds had been turned over. Before we had all gone out to the ablutions we had all carefully laid our kit out ready for inspection. We didn't half curse those stupid little perishers. They both got sent to the Glasshouse over that.

14

Albert Cardwell

Albert's name crops up here and there throughout these notes, which isn't surprising, because apart from Trigger, Albert was my best mate, despite the fact that he sometimes gave me considerable grief. We were together all during training, and right through to the end of the war. Mind you, he wasn't easy to get on with, and he certainly wasn't everyone's cup of tea. As I told you before, he was always in trouble. I used to cover for him as best I could, but he was always on the carpet. You won't be surprised to know that he didn't progress any higher than private.

He was a big chap was Albert, near enough six feet tall, and built like the proverbial brick outhouse. He was very fit, a typical rugby player. His face had more than a few scars, and I don't think that all of them came from playing rugby in St Helens. He could be very aggressive, especially when he had been drinking. Which was quite often. Nevertheless he was a good mate to me, and he would have done anything for me. And I'll tell you one thing, nobody messed with us!

I'll relate a couple of stories about Albert, it will give you a bit of an insight into what he was like. We often used to play cards to pass the time, and most of us became quite good at it. We were playing pontoon one evening, and as was often the case, Albert was losing. I think the other two players were Flash Gorman and Ralph Diamond. Albert was a bad loser, and he was sitting there with a face like thunder. I had a pontoon come up, and cleared the kitty. That was it for Albert, he had no money left. He tried poncing a couple of bob off of the other two, but they didn't want to know. So, he turned to me. 'Come on Pop', he said, 'lend us half a crown.' He already owed me five bob, so I told him to sod off. He stuck his face right into mine, eyeball to eyeball, and asked again. Discretion being the better part of valour, I relented and handed it over. Silly me!

Would you believe it, the jammy so-and-so then proceeded not only to win all his money back, he also cleaned the rest of us out! He wiped the floor with us!

He won five games in a row, and you should have heard him cackle like an old hen as he raked in the money. In the end I was completely skint, so were Flash and Ralph. As we jacked in, Albert very graciously handed back the half crown he owed me. I never did get the five bob!

Albert went to the local pub most nights. If none of us fancied going with him (as was usually the case, because if you went with him and he got into a fight, which was quite often, you would get roped in as well!) or couldn't afford to, he would happily go on his own. One night he got back just before lights out, and as usual, he was a bit the worse for wear. Three sheets to the wind, as they say. He was going round the hut, asking if anyone would bet him two shillings that he couldn't break a broom handle into four-inch lengths. He kept on and on, driving us potty, and in the end some twit accepted the bet just to keep him quiet. That proved to be quite an error of judgement.

There were several brooms in our cleaning cupboard; Albert selected one, pulled the head off, and sat down on his bed. He broke it in half over his knee, and then proceeded to break the two halves, and so on and so on. The task became more and more difficult, he changed knees several times. He showed them to me the next day, they were both red-raw and bruised.

Lights out came and went, but as soon as the sergeant had gone Albert started again, relentless in his task. He was cursing and swearing all the time he was doing it, blokes were shouting at him from all over the room to pack it in, but he took no notice. This went on half the night, and he eventually had six pieces eight inches long. He couldn't break these over his knee, so he tucked them inside his shirt, and climbed up onto one of the metal girders that spanned the width of the hut. He sat up there, banging these pieces of wood on the edge of the girder, bang bang banging away all night. Just as it started to get light, there was a final snap, and he crowed with delight. Oblivious to the hour, he climbed down off the girder, and clutching his twelve pieces of broomstick he marched down the room to confront the poor soul who had taken the bet, and demanded his two shillings!

I could tell you much more about Albert, the fights, the pranks, the drinking, but I think you get the picture. I don't want you to get the wrong idea, he wasn't like this all of the time. He could be generous too, and he was a loyal mate. He never backed out of a fight though, and when we finally went into action, I was glad that he was on our side.

15

Pop Does it Again

We carried on with our training up in the Scottish mountains and as the winter of 1943 arrived we started getting a lot of snow. We often slept out in the open in little bivouacs that slept two, and boy, was it cold! I guess it was an indication of how fit we were that we took it all in our stride.

It was early in December that I received a telegram telling me that I had become a father again. I desperately wanted to get home to see Lily and my new son Michael but I could only get a forty-eight-hour pass. On top of that I had run out of travel warrants. Still, love will find a way as they say, so I scrounged a lift from an army lorry which was going as far as Grantham in Lincolnshire, and then I got a lift from a travelling salesman who took me to Cambridge. Bless his heart, this kind gent treated me to a slap-up lunch. After the meal I started walking along the A10, and as I approached the outskirts of the city an old Austin Seven pulled up and a voice said 'How far are you going, soldier?' The driver was a nurse, and she told me that she was en route to Hoddesdon. 'That'll do me', I told her, and off we went.

When I got to Hoddesdon I caught a 310 bus to Enfield. Because I was in uniform the conductor wouldn't take any money, so I had managed to travel all the way home from Scotland without spending a farthing. What an incredible journey! It was lovely seeing my dear wife and our new little son. I can still picture those two fair heads side by side in our bed. It hadn't been an easy birth, and poor Lily was very tired.

It was also wonderful to see my other two boys, the poor little devils didn't know what was going on. I found out later that they had been told that the midwife had brought the baby in her little black bag! The house was filled with people, I remember Harry being there in his uniform, so he must have been home on leave. Unfortunately I had to go back the next day, so I didn't have very long to get to know my youngest son.

I borrowed some money for the train fare, and believe it or not it took me longer to get back to camp. I was actually late back and was put on a charge, but the old man was sympathetic, and so I escaped any punishment

Billy with Michael, 1943.
Courtesy of Mrs L. Davies.

The Scottish people were wonderful to us. It makes me angry when people speak of the Scots as mean. That certainly wasn't my experience. We moved from Muir of Ord to Glasgow, taking our SPs to an Ordnance depot to be overhauled, repainted, and properly waterproofed. We were billeted at barracks in a place called Cambuslang. Just down the road from us there was a church hall, and some local ladies ran a Servicemen's Club there. We were charged threepence to go in, and this entitled us to numerous cups of tea, and as many sandwiches and cakes as we could eat – all home-made! Each time we went we were given a little gift, things like writing pads, tubes of toothpaste, or tins of boot-polish. We spent a lot of time in that hall with those kind Scots people, playing snooker and table tennis.

There were many places in Glasgow that were off-limits for various reasons, the places I remember in particular were Sauchiehall Street and Pitt Street. Needless to say, these were the very places that the squaddies spent most of their time! Some of us were detailed to act as Regimental Police, and I spent quite a few evenings out on patrol. One evening Albert and I were patrolling Sauchiehall Street, when somebody said that there was a disturbance in a pub. We went along to sort it out, but by the time we got there the trouble was over, and there was only one bloke left in the bar. He was a civilian and was dressed in a light grey suit, and was also wearing a very smart grey trilby hat. At first glance he could have been James Cagney. He was extremely polite, and offered to buy us a drink. While we were sitting chatting to him and drinking our pints I suddenly noticed that poking out of his waistcoat pockets were two ivory-handled cut-throat razors! Discretion being the better part of valour we thanked him for our drinks and beat a very hasty retreat!

It was while we were in Glasgow that I lost my chance for advancement. I was the senior two-striper in the Regiment and was due for promotion, but unfortunately I blew it. This is how it happened. It was Christmas Eve and I was Guard Commander on duty. Lights-out was at 10.30pm, but a lot of the lads were out on a late pass celebrating. It was part of my job to check them in and enter their names in the book as being back by midnight. They all checked in on time except for two soldiers who were supposed to be mates of mine. It was after 1am when they finally turned up and they begged me not to report them. As they were mates I let them go, and to cover myself I made them promise that if they got caught they would report to me first thing in the morning so that I could mark them in the book as being late. Well, they did get caught, by Hector Bennett of all people. They didn't show up in the morning as they had promised, and assuming they had got back without being seen, I marked them in as having got back by midnight. The RSM came and checked the book, and told me that my so-called mates had said that I had let them off because it was Christmas! I was put on a charge and went before my CO Captain Warburton. He said that he was very disappointed in me and that my promotion would be postponed indefinitely. I was relieved, because I thought that I might lose the two stripes I already had! Which all goes to show that if you want to be a sergeant you can't afford to have mates, and you've got to be a bastard!

On Boxing day Albert and I went to Hampden Park to watch an international football match between England and Scotland. We got there late and discovered that the gates had been closed. There was a huge crowd gathered, yelling blue murder, and pressing up against the gates. Suddenly the gates were flung open and the crowd rushed in. We were carried along with the human tide, we couldn't have paid for our tickets if we had wanted to, because we couldn't get our hands out of our pockets! The crowd rushed off to all parts of the ground, and we found a space on the terraces where we were surrounded by Scottish fans. Stanley Matthews, Tom Finney, and Raich Carter were in the English team, and they certainly did us proud. Carter scored a goal within the first five minutes, and we cheered our heads off. This earned us several dirty looks so we thought we'd better tone it down a bit. By half-time Carter had scored a hat-trick. There was stunned silence all around us, and we didn't dare say a word. England went on to win six goals to nil, so you can imagine how we felt walking home with all those disgruntled Scots fans around us. On another occasion we went to Ibrox Park to watch Rangers play Celtic. What an experience that was!

One of my favourite recollections of Scotland is of Albert and I being invited by a family that lived opposite the barracks to join them for the New Year celebrations. As you know, New Year is very important to the Scots, they have all their parties and merry-making then rather than at Christmas. They took us into their homes and treated us like part of their own family, lovely warm-hearted people they were. All the local residents did the same, so all of the lads had a family New Year. Happy memories!

16

The Run-up to D-Day

Well, it was now 1944. We knew that the balloon would be going up soon, and that we would be part of it, but when? We collected our SPs from the Ordnance Depot, and found that they had been painted a different colour. They were now dark green, and on both sides there was a big white star which was the symbol of the Allied forces. On the back and front of each tank there was a black square with a fox's head in the middle, this was now our Brigade badge. We were told that we were now the 8th Armoured Independent Mobile Brigade. What a mouthful! We were attached to the 50th Division. Curiously enough, the Middlesex Regiment, which was my brother-in-law Ned's outfit, was also attached to the 50th Division. Ned and I often fought the same battles, but we never came across each other.

Our role was to be an independent mobile force which could move quickly to any area of battle where support was needed. This was what all those months of training had been about! We stayed in Glasgow through until April, and then the rumours started flying about that something big was about to happen. We were all called to attend a lecture about the need for secrecy, and this just confirmed our suspicions. We all started to get really excited, action at last! We were keen to get stuck in, although it was beginning to dawn on us that this time the fighting would be for real.

Early in May our SPs were loaded onto tank transporters, and off we set for a destination that was known only to the CO. We travelled down the East Coast and spent the first night of our journey at a caravan site in Bridlington. The next day we made it to Grantham, and after a hard slog we reached Beaulieu in the New Forest. We were staying in a huge tented camp, known as Camp B6; there were thousands upon thousands of tents. The whole show was being run by the American army. We were told that it was a sealed camp, and that no one was allowed in or out. We now knew for certain that this was it.

The food was good, and we were allowed plenty of time off. The Yanks still ran their gambling operations in a huge marquee; all we could afford to do was

A Sherman tank with D Troop. With TR. Courtesy of Frank Holt.

Sherman tank with D Troop. Courtesy of Frank Holt.

just stand there and watch. We knew that we wouldn't be getting paid for a long time. Our days were spent in attending lectures, revising most of our previous training, and also preparing our SPs for action. We stripped and cleaned all of our weapons, loaded up with ammunition and supplies, and generally got ourselves and our equipment ready for what was to come.

We were all nervous, but some of the blokes really panicked when they realised they would soon be going into action. We heard that a number of soldiers had inflicted various injuries on themselves just to get their ticket. One of our own blokes, a lad called Steve Count, had actually dropped a tank bogie wheel on his foot, hoping to hurt himself enough to get sent to hospital. The most he expected was a couple of broken bones, but he miscalculated and took his foot clean off. What a price to pay!

We spent most of the next fortnight talking about what would happen when we went into action. We knew that we were going to invade France, but when? And where? A lot of the troops were getting on edge, and none of us liked all the hanging about. We wanted to get on with it. We all had our hair cut really short, talk about skinheads! I remember thinking, 'Trigger would have hated this!' We underwent rigorous medical examinations, and were given all the usual inoculations for going abroad. We had to hand over all our personal property for safe-keeping in case we were taken prisoner. All we were allowed to keep was one photograph of your wife or girlfriend, or if you were single, your mother. The only other thing we were allowed to keep was our dog-tags.

Then came the great day! Or so we thought. We drove down to Buckler's Hard where we loaded our SPs onto LCTs. We had already loaded up with ammunition and rations, and just before we left we topped up our fuel tanks, with another sixty gallons in the Jerry cans strapped to the back. We sailed into the Solent and anchored just off of Lymington. When we looked around us we were absolutely astounded at the number of vessels around us. It was a magnificent sight, hundreds and hundreds of ships. Besides the LCTs there were motor torpedo boats, cruisers, destroyers, battleships, aircraft carriers, and merchant ships of all kinds. How on earth the Germans didn't know we were coming is something that will always remain a mystery to me.

We thought we were just going to sail straight off, but apparently the weather was too bad. It was pretty foul, raining buckets. We were all feeling somewhat miserable, and the weather didn't help matters. We were told that we would probably be sailing on 5 June which was two days later, but it seemed like forever. Our living quarters were very basic, in fact I was sleeping in the engine room, and I couldn't get the stink of diesel out of my nostrils.

Now, I still can't quite believe I did what I'm just about to tell you. It was incredibly risky, and incredibly foolhardy, but it just goes to show you the kind of things you do when you're young and foolish and in love. I don't think I'd have had the bottle to do it on my own. A lot of us married blokes had been talking about our families, and how we were desperate to see them before we shipped out. I was thinking about Lily and the boys all the time, and it was breaking my heart to think how she would react when she knew I had gone into action. A mate of mine named Bert Sherriff came to see me and said that he was determined to see his wife one more time before we left. I don't know to this day how on earth he arranged it, but this is the story. He had bribed someone to leave a rowing boat tied up next to our LCT, and asked if I wanted to jump ship with him to go and see my family. The idea scared me stiff, but I knew that I might never see Lily or the boys again, so I decided to chance it.

During the very early hours the next morning we slipped over the side and rowed like mad for the shore which was about half a mile away. We beached the boat and pulled it up into some bushes. Then we walked up to a nearby road and waited for a while, and before too long a three-ton truck came along. Seeing us in uniform the driver pulled up and we jumped on board. He took us all the way to Uxbridge and dropped us off outside the Underground station. We caught a tube train on the Piccadilly line, and Bert got off at Finsbury Park. I went on to Enfield West (Now Oakwood) and caught a bus home. Poor Lily's face was a picture as she answered the door. Of course she was delighted to see me, but I think that when she first saw me she must have thought that I had deserted.

I could only stay for half an hour, but it was worth it to see my lovely girl and our boys. My mind was in turmoil, and I guess hers was too. I can still picture little Billy goggling up at this apparition in uniform who was kissing his Mummy! We said our farewells; Lily was really upset, but she put on a brave face.

I had arranged to meet Bert that evening at Victoria, but again I was skint, so I had to cadge the fare off of Lily. To be honest, I had thought of not going back at all, but even though I was scared witless I still had this feeling that I couldn't let my mates down. I got to Victoria and saw all the Redcaps prowling around, so I hid myself in a toilet until it was time for the train to leave. I couldn't find Bert anywhere, but I guessed that he was out there somewhere.

There were hundreds of soldiers milling around all over the station, and I thought they must all be doing the same as me. The time came for the train to leave and there was one mad rush for the barrier. The ticket collectors and the Redcaps were just brushed aside. Some of the soldiers were caught, but the majority (including me!) got through. The train was actually moving when I jumped on, and I only just made it. I was lucky enough to find an empty toilet, and I locked myself in. I stayed in there until the train was coming in to Brockenhurst. I opened the door and stood there, waiting for the train to slow down as it got near the station, and as it did so I chucked all my gear out and jumped. So did about twenty other blokes! We all disappeared into the undergrowth, and with some difficulty I found my way back to where we had left the boat.

While I was blundering about in the bushes I was hoping fervently that Bert hadn't gone off without me, but when I got to the hiding place, there was the boat. There was no sign of Bert, so I sat down and waited. And waited. And waited. I started to get a bit anxious and wondered if I should go off without him. Suddenly, after what seemed like hours, there was a low whistle, and Bert appeared out of the gloom. We dragged the boat back to the water's edge, threw our stuff in, and started to row out to the waiting fleet. By now it had turned midnight, and it was pitch-black. We couldn't really see where we were going, and like a couple of berks we hadn't thought to take the number of our LCT. Let me tell you that in the dark, one naval vessel looks very much like another. We rowed round and round, not daring to make a sound or call out, but we simply had no way of finding our LCT. Just as we were getting really desperate a familiar voice rang out, 'Who goes there?' There was no mistaking that Scouse accent, it was my old mate Albert! Bless his heart, he was on guard duty and had seen us floundering about. I could have kissed him! We pulled alongside, and Albert helped me to scramble on board. I scuttled off to my quarters, but unfortunately for Bert he bumped into an officer who was taking a stroll around the deck. He tried to bluff his way out of it, but the game was up.

The next day Bert was up before Captain Sidgewick, and to my shame and embarrassment I was detailed as one of his escorts! As it happened, there wasn't much that the CO could do in the way of punishment, so all Bert got was seven days' pay stopped. Like a good mate he didn't give me away, and I thanked my lucky stars that I had got away with it. What you might call a bit of an adventure – a nice one though!

17

We're Going in!

The next couple of days and nights were a nightmare of anticipation. The weather was still atrocious on 5 June, and we were told that the exercise had been cancelled.

[Editor's note: The Supreme Commander General Eisenhower took considerable notice of the weather conditions. In *Gold Beach Jig* by Tim Saunders the following extract from his notes is quoted: 'At 3.30 am the next morning (5 June) our little camp was shaking and shuddering under a wind of almost hurricane proportions and the accompanying rain seemed to be travelling in horizontal streaks. When the conference started the first report given to us by Group Captain Stagg was that the bad conditions predicted were actually prevailing … their next astonishing declaration was that by the following morning a period of relatively good weather, heretofore completely unexpected, would ensue, lasting probably thirty-six hours.']

It was playing havoc with our nerves but that very evening the fleet started sailing out of the Solent. Operation Overlord was under way! Once we got out into the open sea it was very rough. A lot of the troops had a miserable time being seasick, the damn pills they gave us weren't worth a light. At 1 am the Captain called us all together for a briefing. He told us that we would be landing on a stretch of the French coast code-named Gold Beach, the actual location was a little village called Le Hamel, just outside of Arromanches.

[Editor's note: A further quote from *Gold Beach Jig* reads: '231 Brigade's Intelligence Summary lists the defences at Le Hamel as follows: "The defences of Le Hamel consisted of three strong points; the first covering the exit onto JIG Green, the second covering the ramp onto the beach at the centre of the sea-front and the third covering the exit and beach to the west. Le Hamel EAST: the strong point covering the exit from the beaches consists of two MG pill-boxes, also a concrete shelter surmounted by a cupola, sited on top of the ramp, and possibly mounting an anti-tank or infantry gun. A communication trench with open MG emplacements leads to another MG pill-box just to the EAST. All round defence for this position is afforded by a pill-box and several weapons pits with communication trenches sited in gardens, on the west side of the road leading from the ramp.'"]

We would make landfall at 6 am and our task was to support the assault force, which was made up of British Commandos. He then told us that our journey would take a few hours yet, and that we should take the opportunity to get our heads down. Sleep! I ask you, how could we sleep? My heart was pounding like a steam-hammer. We just sat around and talked, and some of us exchanged addresses and promised that we would contact each others' families if we didn't make it. [See General Richardson's notes on D-Day.]

Suddenly we heard the roar of aircraft, hundreds of them, flying towards the coast. Even though it was dark we could still see them. After a while we heard the sound of bombs being dropped and the horizon suddenly lit up like bonfire night. It went on for ages, and as dawn broke we saw several huge columns of smoke rising. Just then the battleships and cruisers started an artillery barrage. The noise was appalling, we had to shout to hear one another. I remember thinking, 'Didn't the CO tell us to get some sleep?' Alongside us were LCTs that had been adapted as rocket launchers, and they opened up, adding to the din.

Aircraft of all descriptions were still passing by overhead, and we saw big Liberator bombers towing gliders. In the distance we saw two planes get hit, and suddenly there were parachutes opening up and floating down into the sea. All this time the weather was getting worse, and the waves were getting bigger. We saw an LCT, not far from us, rise into the air, and as it came down it broke in half. Some of the troops and crew were picked up by rescue boats, but I'll bet most of the poor buggers were drowned! As we got nearer to the French coast we saw landing craft filled with Commandos being lowered into the sea. As they made for shore the German batteries opened up, and we saw several of them disappear under the water.

[Editor's note: Tim Saunders records the thoughts of Major Wernher Pluskat who was 'standing to' in his battle position: 'Hardly a word was spoken between us in the bunker, but the tension was increasing all the time. As the first grey light of dawn began to creep across the sky I thought I could see something along the horizon. I picked up my artillery binoculars and stepped back with amazement when I saw that the horizon was literally filling with ships of all kinds. I could hardly believe it. It seemed to me impossible that this vast fleet could have gathered without anyone knowing. I passed the binoculars to the man alongside me and said "Take a look." He replied, "My God, it's the invasion."']

We knew it would be our turn to go soon, and sure enough the order was given for us to take post. We exchanged 'This is it!' looks, and climbed on board our SP. We also started firing, but the pitch and toss of the boat didn't help our accuracy much. Still, we were only too glad to be doing something. We got closer and closer to the shore, and all at once there was the sound of bullets pinging and clanging on the side of our boat. A German fighter plane screamed over the top of us, he was being chased by a Spitfire. The Jerry was hit and started giving off black smoke. We cheered our heads off; one or two of the lads started giggling, no doubt through nerves.

The Navy ramp crew took up their positions, so we knew that we would soon be going ashore. We were all busy keeping our heads down when all of a sudden there was an almighty explosion. The bows of our boat simply disappeared, and so did the poor sailors. We had hit a mine! The Jerries had put steel girders in the water just under the surface, and had fixed mines on the ends. It was one of these that we had hit. [Editor's note: From *Gold Beach Jig*, a description of typical rudimentary tank-traps as described by Oberstleutnant Fritz Ziegleman, Chief of Staff 352nd Division: 'Assuming that the enemy landings would only take place at high tide, obstacles of all kinds were erected on the top part of the beach, so that their upper parts projected from the sea. 'Tsechen' hedgehog defences, pile-driven stakes of metal and concrete, as well as wooden trestles were set up here and partly charged with deep water or surface mines and high explosives.'] Thank goodness we didn't sink, but when we grounded a few minutes later in four feet of water, we didn't know how we were going to get all the tanks and other vehicles off. It was too steep to just go over the edge.

One of our officers, Lieutenant Cook, then had a brainwave. He jumped into the Bren-gun carrier that was due to be the first vehicle off, and drove it over the edge. When it had sunk we were able to use it as a stepping stone, and the SPs started to roll off. When it was our turn we drove like mad for the beach.

A beach near Le Hamel (where the Essex Yeomanry came ashore), D-Day. Courtesy of www. thedonovan.com

There were explosions going off all around us as shells landed, some of them were German, and a lot of them were ours! We were under fire from German machine gun posts and we could hear the bullets clanging on the outside of our SP. The driver's compartment filled up with water, poor old Flash Gorman was up to his waist in it. So much for the water-proofing!

We were almost ashore when there was an almighty bang from our rear, and we came to a halt. The force of the explosion gave us all slight concussion, and it took us a few minutes to recover. We had been hit by an artillery round which had destroyed our engine. What happened next was terrible. Our tank commander Sergeant Bill Wilby [see Notes on the Text] decided to have a look over the side to inspect the damage. I think he must still have been concussed, because I don't think that otherwise he would have done it. He suddenly fell back into the well of the SP. His face was horribly grey, and it took us a few seconds to realise that he was dead. We were stunned, and for a while we just didn't know what to do next. The lads were all looking expectantly at me, and it dawned on me that I was now the senior soldier. I decided that we would all stay put for the time being. By this time we were all starving hungry. We hadn't eaten since we left England. So, despite poor old Bill lying there, we opened a tin of bully beef and broke out some hard tack.

Just as we were settling down to eat there was a fearful banging on the side of our SP. 'Bloody hell', I thought, 'What now?' So, I very gingerly looked over the side, and I saw one of those steel girders that I mentioned earlier. It was being washed up against our tracks by the waves, and to my horror, I saw that stuck on the end of it was a dirty great mine! 'There's only one thing to do,' I thought, 'Run!' Then common sense clicked in – there were still shells exploding all around us, and you could still hear the buzz of bullets flying around like angry bees. So, we were better off staying where we were. Still, that mine would have to be dealt with. So Ralphie Diamond and I jumped over the side and very carefully grabbed hold of the whole shebang and carried it a few yards up the beach. We stuck it back in the sand and then we dashed back and climbed into the SP. Phew! That was dodgy!

We stayed there for a few hours, and by midday things were quietening down a bit. There were still shells falling here and there, but not so many bullets. I told the lads to gather up our small-arms, and as much grub as they could carry, and to follow me to the sea-wall. We also took a spade, and after a frantic dash we dug a hole in the sand right up against the wall, and jumped in. We hadn't been there long when a loud voice shouted, 'OK you men, follow me!' The owner of the voice was a remarkable character. He was a naval officer, and I noticed that he had one arm missing. He was accompanied by of all things, a bulldog on a lead. He was one of the beach-masters, and he led us along the beach and handed us over to a

Royal Engineers Sergeant Major. After we told the latter what had happened to us he said that our regiment had gone inland. He said that they would send someone back for us, but in the meantime, we were to be at his disposal.

Left: Coiffant un pieu metallique. Courtesy of www.6juin1944.com

Below: SP of A Troop at H-Hour + 60 watching the 50th Northumberland Infantry disembarking from an LCI. Courtesy of the Essex Yeomanry.

18

Make Yourselves Useful Lads!

We stood there scratching our heads, wondering what we would have to do. We soon found out, and the real horror of the landing was beginning to unfold. The tide had started to go out, and all along the beach, as far as the eye could see in either direction there were masses of dead bodies. Hundreds upon hundreds of them. Among the dead there were countless numbers of poor sods who were terribly injured. Our first job was to rescue them and take them back to a retrieval point. All the time this was going on there were still troops and vehicles pouring ashore from landing craft and LCTs, and as the boats were emptied we loaded them with some of the wounded. We also had to bring in the dead bodies and line them up for identification. We used the same stretchers for both jobs, and for hours we struggled backwards and forwards through the soft sand and laid our poor dead comrades head to toe along the beach road.

Later on that evening we got a break, and we walked along the rows of bodies to see if we could identify any of our mates. As I lifted the blanket off of one face I saw that blood was spurting out of the poor lad's mouth, so I called a medic over. He told us that the boy was still alive and they carried him off to the field hospital. I have often wondered what happened to him.

Before long a regiment of the Pioneer Corps turned up and started gathering up the dead. We were truly thankful to be relieved of that unhappy duty. We watched the Mulberry Dock being built, a marvellous floating harbour, we were amazed at the speed with which the Royal Engineers completed it. As soon as it was in place even more troops, vehicles, tanks and field guns came pouring in, it seemed like an endless stream.

When it got dark we thankfully returned to our hole in the sand and bedded down for the night. No peace for the wicked though, just after midnight we were woken by the RE Sergeant Major and he told us to follow him again. He took us to where an army chaplain was waiting in a jeep. Parked behind the jeep was a three-ton truck. This officer told us that we were going to a village three

Above: Sword Beach on D-Day. Courtesy of
www.britannica.com

Left: A Teller Mine atop a stake. Courtesy of www.army.mil

miles up the line. Our mission was to pick up some wounded soldiers and bring
them back to the beachhead. Nothing to it, I thought. Three of the lads went in
the jeep with the Padre, and the rest of us followed in the truck, with Flash as
driver. It wasn't easy driving in the dark with no lights, but we managed.

We soon reached the outskirts of the village, and we were flagged down by
an infantry officer. He spoke to the padre, and after a while we were called
over for a briefing. We were told that the wounded men were in a school hall
in the middle of the village. The officer also told us that the Germans were
holding the other end of the village. The padre said that he didn't think that

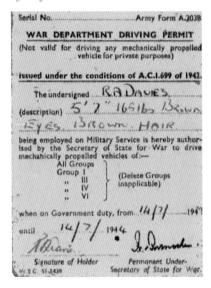

Serial No. .... Army Form A.2038

WAR DEPARTMENT DRIVING PERMIT

(Not valid for driving any mechanically propelled vehicle for private purposes)

issued under the conditions of A.C.I.699 of 1942

The undersigned R.A DAVIES

(description) 5'7" 165lbs Brown EYES. BROWN HAIR

being employed on Military Service is hereby authorised by the Secretary of State for War to drive mechanically propelled vehicles of:—

All Groups
Group I
" III   } (Delete Groups
" IV   } inapplicable)
" VI

when on Government duty, from 14/7/ 194

until 14/7/ 1944

Signature of Holder   Permanent Under-Secretary of State for War.
W.S.C. 51.3439

A driving permit. Courtesy of Mrs L. Davies.

they would shoot at us because he had a red cross painted on either side of his jeep. I pointed out that we had no red cross painted on the side of the truck, but he insisted that we would be safe, so off we set. Flash made a great job of backing the truck into a very narrow gateway, and we helped to get the wounded on board.

There were twenty-four of them altogether, too many for one journey. It was decided that some of the more seriously wounded would have to be left behind. The journey back over rough terrain would probably have killed some of them anyway. Once we had a full load we drove hell for leather back to the coast, and to our relief, the Germans didn't fire on us. The padre had been right. The next morning we were assigned to the same chaplain again, only this time we took a load of ammunition with us. Bit crafty, I suppose. Three times that day we made the same trip, and each time we took ammo up the line and brought wounded back. One of my abiding memories is the cries and groans of agony from the poor blokes as we went over bumps in the road. When we got back to the beach we loaded them onto LCTs which ferried them out to the hospital ship. Jokingly, I told the lads that I was thinking of going with them, and Ralph Diamond said, 'What, and miss all the fun Pop?' I was to remember those words later on.

Later on that day we went looking for a better hole to make our home in, and we came across an abandoned German bunker. It had been damaged quite extensively by shellfire, but one end of it was reasonably habitable, so we started to clear it out and move our kit in. As we were doing so there was a horrible stench, so we dug down a bit and found a dead Jerry, he looked like just a kid. Anyway, we got rid of him and settled in. For the first time since we had landed we got a fire going, and brewed up some tea. The tea was bloody awful, but it was wet and warm, it went down a treat! That night we actually got a full night's sleep, despite the indescribable noise going on all around us. Somehow we were getting used to it.

We woke early the next morning to the sound of a dogfight going on above us. It was one hell of a scrap between a Spitty and a German fighter, and after a while the Jerry plane caught fire. The pilot baled out, and we watched him float down in the middle of a field behind us, and it was obvious that he didn't know it was a minefield! He landed OK, and as we watched he stripped off his flying suit and just stood there in his magnificent Luftwaffe uniform. A couple of Royal Engineers shouted to him to stay where he was and that they would come to get him. He either didn't hear them or he didn't understand, or perhaps he just didn't care. He just stood to attention for a few seconds, and then he marched straight forward. We all crouched down and put our fingers in ears, but he must have had a charmed life because he came through unscathed. As he was taken away he had a huge grin on his face.

There was a further bit of excitement that day; we heard some shouting from the beach and it sounded as if somebody was in trouble. We rushed down to the shore and saw a Sherman tank about a hundred yards out in the water. Only the turret was showing, and perched on the top was a young soldier. I called out to him, and he shouted back that the water was too deep and that he couldn't swim. It was fairly rough, so we couldn't get to him, but there were some naval types milling around in a dinghy further out. We called out to them, telling them to go and rescue him. The silly sod didn't see them coming, and he jumped in and started thrashing about. The sailors had already started making their way towards him, and eventually they grabbed him and hauled him on board. By the time they got him to shore he was in a bad way. He had swallowed a fair amount of the English Channel, but we pumped it out of him and by the time the medics arrived he had started to recover. Thank goodness!

We went back to our cosy little bunker and had some more bully beef and beans, and just as we were finishing our meal a familiar voice called out, 'is that all you've got to do, Bombardier Davies?' And there on the road above us was our Adjutant, Major Dick Gosling. [See Notes on the Text.] He was standing up in a Bren-gun carrier. He had come back for us! He told us that he had been looking for us all day, and that we were to be issued with a new SP at a nearby Ordnance depot. We loaded up all our gear and he took us back to the regiment. We were given quite a welcome, many of the lads thought we had bought it.

19

Further into France

I had to report to Captain Sidgewick on our activities during those three missing days. He was very sad to hear that Bill had been killed, and told me that I was to take over as number one on our crew. He said that I had shown good leadership qualities, but he still couldn't promote me because of my previous reprimand. So, I was the only tank commander in the regiment who wasn't at least a sergeant. Our replacement SP was ready to be collected, and the ordnance boys had tanked her up and loaded her with ammo. When we went to the Ordnance Depot to pick her up I was shown our old SP. It had been hit in the engine compartment and it looked for all the world as if a damn great hole had been drilled through the armour plating. The shell had churned up that great big engine as if it had been mincemeat. It had missed the petrol tanks by inches; how we had avoided being blown up I'll never know. I thought to myself, 'Someone up there must be looking after me.'

We needed a replacement crew member, and after a while a young fellow named Ned Spry was allocated to us. He was a nice lad, very timid, he didn't say much, but he was good at his job. The regiment was camped just outside a village by the name of Villers Bocage. It was a pretty little place, surrounded by beautiful countryside. It seemed such a shame to me that it should be desecrated by all the trappings of war.

Not far from the village there was a wooded hill, we knew it as Hill 103. On top of this hill the German Army had a very big gun, I reckon it was at least a 9.2 inch. Try as they might, our infantry were having a hell of a job to get rid of it. The hill was being defended by three Tiger tanks, and between them they were inflicting terrible casualties on our boys. The Tiger tank was formidable, it was heavily armoured, and the front of its superstructure was 150mm thick. It had an eighty-eight millimetre gun which could do a heck of a lot of damage, it was easily the best weapon in the German arsenal. Took a lot of knocking out, did a Tiger.

We deployed at the bottom of the hill and tried some long-range shooting, but this was largely ineffective. However, we had the advantage, because the Tigers couldn't depress their guns low enough to fire directly at us. A squadron of British Sherman tanks outflanked them while our Sextons fired at them over open sights. Eventually we destroyed them, but not without cost. I lost a lot of good mates in that little shindig. When we got to the top of the hill we discovered that our infantry had captured the big gun and had also taken a lot of prisoners.

We pushed on to the outskirts of Caen, and soon found ourselves on the high ground which looks down on the town. As it began to get dark we saw British bombers flying over the town, and we could hear all the air-raid sirens going off. It made me think about Lily and our boys, and all the folks at home. No doubt they were hearing air-raid sirens too!

SP B2 (Brentwood) 413 Battery near Nijmegen, 21 September 1944. Courtesy of the Essex Yeomanry.

The reason for our attack on Caen was to check the advance of the German Panzer Divisions. If we could hold up most of them up, it would allow the Yanks to sweep through further south. As the dawn came up we could see in the distance the long white vapour trails of V2 rockets which had been launched towards Britain. That made us think, I can tell you! We had already seen a couple of launch pads for the V1 flying bombs, nicknamed 'Doodle-bugs' which had caused so much damage on London.

Our CO called all the officers and tank commanders together and told us that we had been ordered to support a regiment of Yanks in one particular sector. Apparently they were having a rough time and their morale was low. We made our way down to the Saint Lo area; our brief was to rendezvous with this American unit which was holed up in a large orchard. The idea was that we would take over from them so that they could be withdrawn for a rest. Unfortunately it didn't work out like that! By the time we got there it was getting dark, but we could just about make out some movement in the orchard. Unsuspecting, we drove straight in, and can you imagine our horror when we came under fire! What we didn't know was that the Yanks had done a bunk without letting anyone know, and the Germans had moved in! We had to make a run for it, but of course we took hell of a battering. We lost three SPs, and quite a few blokes got killed. Our CO was furious, and so were we. This was by no means the only time we lost blokes through American incompetence. As you will see!

After this incident we needed to recoup our losses, and we were sent back to a rest camp in Bayeux. We stayed there for three days while the regiment was brought back up to strength. Bayeux was a beautiful place despite all the bomb damage it had suffered. I particularly remember the Cathedral. This was my first glimpse of French life. I loved the old-fashioned buildings and the narrow cobbled streets. They had open-air toilets called 'Pissoirs'. It took a bit of getting used to, anyone passing by could see what you were doing! There was a river running through the town and I remember that there was a sign on one of the bridges which said 'Defense de pisser dans la Rivière'. It amused me to see that this sign was still there when I went back to Bayeux fifty years later!

The rest camp was excellent, it was wonderful to be able to have a bath and change our underclothes. It was a luxury to be able to sit at a table to eat, and off a decent plate! While we were there we were entertained by Gracie Fields and George Formby. I heard afterwards that George had insisted on going up to the front line where he sang to the troops from the tailgate of a lorry. They loved him for that.

After the three days were up we were on the move again, this time towards Falaise. You will have read in your history books about something called 'The Falaise Gap'. This was a narrow corridor of land into which the Jerries were being pushed by the Allies. They were hemmed in on both sides and sooner or later they would have to try to break out. They were being bombed and strafed night and day by Allied planes as well as being shelled by our artillery. Nonetheless they were tough these Jerries, and they held on for quite some time. As a result our advance came to a bit of a standstill at a tiny village in the Normandy countryside. It wasn't exactly a village, more of a hamlet. It was called Thury Harcourt.

We had begun to get a bit bored with army rations, bully beef, hard tack, and those terrible compo rations. Every regiment had one or two blokes who were born scroungers, scouring the neighbouring villages and farms for fresh meat, vegetables, eggs, and the like. Ours was no exception. The best scrounger I ever met was a fellow named Jimmy Duffield. He came from somewhere up north, and was blessed with the gift of the gab. He always had this big grin on his face and he could talk the hind leg off a donkey. While we were at Thury Harcourt I had the privilege (and I do consider it a privilege!) of going with him on one of his scrounging expeditions, and I can tell you that it was quite educational to see him in action.

Armed with a couple of bars of chocolate and a few packets of Wills Woodbines we set off to find the local farms and cottages. We had a few words of French, but mostly we communicated by pointing and sign language. We stopped at one charming little cottage and knocked on the door. When it opened we were faced by a typical-looking French farm worker, complete with smock and beret. With our rudimentary French we managed to convey to him that we wanted things such as eggs, cheese, ham, and bread. That was OK, and before long we had all of those things, and then Jimmy asked him for some fat to fry the eggs in. We couldn't make him understand, so we pantomimed frying eggs, and even tried to make noises like bacon frying, then all of a sudden our Frenchman burst out laughing. With a distinct cockney accent he said 'Do you boys want some dripping?' We were absolutely flabbergasted, we had been completely taken in. He explained to us that he had served in the British Army during the First World War, and that he had fallen in love with a French girl. They had married, and he had settled down here in Normandy. What a lovely story! We didn't realise it, but we had struck gold!

That particular part of Normandy is famous for its cider, and for a very strong type of apple brandy called Calvados. Most of the local farmers had stills, and thank goodness our cockney Frenchman was one of them. He took us to a well and wound up the windlass, and we saw to our delight that on the end of the hook there was a great big barrel of Calvados! He told us that he had hidden the barrel down the well so that the Germans wouldn't steal it. He asked us if we wanted some, so I rushed off back to our camp and picked up an empty water can. We were now the proud owners of four and a half gallons of firewater!

We took our booty back to camp and shared it out. Our share was half a gallon. Boy, was it potent! The food was used to supplement our army issue rations. In addition to the food we could scrounge from farms we used to get the odd rabbit or chicken, it all made mealtimes a bit more bearable. Let me enlighten you a bit about army rations. I've mentioned compo rations, an example of this was the tea. Processed tea, milk, and sugar were compressed into a small cube, something like an oxo cube, and you just put it in a mug and poured boiling water on it. It tasted awful, and its only saving grace was that it was wet and warm! The rations came in small wooden boxes marked with the letters A through to G. We would get the A pack on a Sunday, the B pack on the Monday and so on. Naturally the A pack was the best, it contained tinned steak and kidney pudding, tinned spotted dick with instant custard, and tinned ham and bully beef. The other packs had a variety of tinned stews or minced meat, and every pack contained dehydrated potatoes, tinned peas, baked beans, and tins of fruit. There was a bag of boiled sweets per week for each man, along with a small bar of chocolate and a tin of fifty Capstan cigarettes.

We also had Iron Rations. These consisted of hardtack biscuits and a block of chocolate which contained things like vegetable and meat concentrate. It tasted awful, but it would keep you going in an emergency. There were vitamin pills on hand to supplement this very basic diet. So you can see why we liked to get some ordinary food whenever we could!

Unfortunately it didn't always follow that we would get the 'treats' contained in our ration boxes. Time and time again I remember opening them and finding items missing. Some of the rotten buggers at the Supply Depot used to break into the rations and steal the best things like the bars of chocolate, sweets, and cigarettes and sell them off to the locals. I've often thought that there are probably a lot of men around who became rich by robbing their mates during the war. I wonder if their consciences ever prick them. They should!

We had a rather unique method of cooking the fresh food that we scrounged. We had these big square five gallon petrol tins which we would cut in half. We filled one half with earth, poured neat aviation fuel on it, and when we lit it, it would burn for ages. The other half of the tin was used as a cooking pot. We would just put anything we had to hand in the pot and let it simmer away. It might be rabbit, or sometimes a chicken, and all sorts of vegetables. Of course we could only eat like that when we were out of action. During a battle it was back to bully beef and biscuits.

It was getting on for late August, and it seemed as if we were never going to break out of the bridgehead. To be frank, we had started to get a bit bored. All we had to do to occupy ourselves was to clean our equipment, and sit around chewing the fat and playing cards during our breaks. Then, one Sunday morning, we were called together for a Drumhead service. Our chaplain led us in prayers to God for victory. I sometimes reflected that a few miles down the road there was probably a German chaplain leading German troops in similar prayers. And if that were the case, which side would God favour? It takes some thinking about, doesn't it? A briefing for the tank commanders followed the service, and we were told that the Big Push was to start the next morning at dawn, on 26 August.

I was on guard duty that evening, and unbeknown to me my crew decided to take on a bit of Dutch courage. They broke open the Calvados and started knocking it back. By the time I got off duty, they were well away. I was furious! They knew damn well that I was on probation, and of course it was my duty to ensure that they stayed clear-headed for the battle to come. The most inebriated was Flash, our driver. He was absolutely legless! I spent most of that night trying to sober him up, but it was hopeless. The other lads told me that he had been guzzling Calvados by the mugful. Try as we might, we couldn't rouse him from his drunken stupor. I began to worry that he had drunk himself to death! At 5 am the artillery barrage started up, and the air was filled with the noise of hundreds of big guns going off. We got the order to move out, and Flash was still unconscious. I had no alternative but to drive the bloody SP myself! So, I put his hat on and set off, hoping to Christ that none of the officers would notice. With the noise of the barrage, the drone of hundreds of aircraft flying overhead, and the noise of our powerful engine, I had great difficulty in concentrating on the driving and trying to listen to my orders on the radio at the same time. I was cursing Flash every yard I drove, calling him every name under the sun, but he didn't care, he was oblivious to the lot, his inert body rolling around in the well of the SP. Thankfully we came to a halt, and the order was received to commence firing. This was what we did most of the day, creeping forward, and then stopping and firing off a few rounds.

The so-called Falaise Gap was getting narrower and narrower, and the Germans were suffering terrible losses. With our attack, heavily supported by artillery and air bombardment, we really had them on the run. When we got into Falaise we started to realise just how badly they had suffered. There were wrecked vehicles of all kinds, some of them still burning. There were dead horses and cattle in the fields, but the most horrible sight was the thousands of dead German soldiers. That memory will haunt me for the rest of my days. There were bodies everywhere, and at one point the road was so congested with them that we couldn't get by. They had to be bulldozed out of the way. It made me feel sick. In fact, many of the lads did lose their breakfast.

We continued chasing the Germans up the road; we went on for miles, the High Command didn't want them to have a chance to rally and offer any kind of resistance. We did get one break, and we pulled off the road and got the tea brewing. To our relief Flash had now recovered from his binge of the night before, although he was suffering from one hell of a hangover. 'Serves the bastard right!' I thought. Mind you, it taught him a lesson, and as far as I can recall he never got that pie-eyed again.

20

On into Belgium and Holland

The crew started to prepare a meal by the roadside and I stayed on board to keep a look-out, scanning the land on both sides of the road with my binoculars. We were in a valley; the farmer's fields sloped upwards and were dotted here and there with trees, hedges, and bushes. I spotted movement behind one of the bushes, and at first I thought it was a farm animal, but then I made out the field-grey uniform of a German soldier. I raised the alarm, and Lieutenant Cook led a squad of armed men up the hill. As they approached the bushes the Germans stood up and raised their arms in surrender. There were at least a hundred of them. They were lined up on the road, and I must say they looked a sorry lot. The youngest of them only looked about fifteen, and some of the older blokes must have been over sixty. The food we found in their haversacks was horrible German sausage and black rye bread which was all wet and soggy in the middle.

The Captain congratulated me for spotting them, and said that as a reward I could have the privilege of marching the prisoners back to the Military Police Depot in the town of Gace. 'Lucky me', I thought. A corporal named Tom Crabtree was detailed to come with me, and armed with a Sten-gun each we set off with this motley crew to escort them into captivity.

We marched them off down the road and we'd gone about two miles when we were joined by a scruffy bunch of armed civilians. They belonged to the Maquis, the French Resistance, and they begged us to hand our prisoners over to them. I had a pretty good idea of what would happen to the unfortunate Germans if I agreed, and I wasn't having any of it. Besides which, I would most certainly have been on the carpet. So, we just ignored them, but they marched every step of the way with us, murder on their faces, and the tension was almost unbearable. God knows what some of those German boys must have been thinking.

We reached Gace at last, and as we marched along the main street, the local people turned out in their hundreds, jeering and spitting, and throwing stones at the Jerries. We reached the Military Police Depot and handed the prisoners over, much to our relief. As we did so, Tom and I were surrounded by French people, all shouting and cheering, and patting us on the back. We were practically carried along to the Mayor's house, he was bowing and scraping to us, and gabbling away, we couldn't understand a word, but we got the message that he was offering us the town's hospitality.

He invited us into his humble home for a meal and a drink. All sorts of people turned up, wine was flowing, and the affair turned into a full-blown party. Before long it was too late for us to make our way back to the Regiment, so the Mayor insisted that we spend the night in his house. He even gave up his bed for us! The next morning we reported to the Military Police, and they gave us a lift back to the Regiment. We found that our boys had moved on in our absence, they were now in a new location a few miles further on, just outside a town called L'Aigle.

Later that day there was a terrible incident, and two of my best mates were killed. The tragedy was, there wasn't a German in sight! We had pulled into a farmyard for a rest and a brew-up, when suddenly a flight of aircraft screamed overhead. We didn't take too much notice, because we could clearly see that they

B Troop with liberated civilians. Courtesy of the Essex Yeomanry.

were on our side. They were Mitchell bombers of the American Air Force. Some of the lads even waved. The planes circled round, and then dived straight at us. To our horror, we saw their bombs being released and realised that we were the target. As the bombs screamed down most of us dived for cover under the SPs. However, two of our crew, Ralph Diamond and the youngster Ned Spry ran into a barn [see Notes on the Text]. As they did so it sustained a direct hit, and exploded in flames. When the bombers flew off we rushed over to what was left of the barn. Ned had been killed instantly, and poor old Ralph was badly wounded. He died later on that day.

It's difficult to tell you how I felt, I don't mind admitting that I cried buckets. I was absolutely shattered. Ralph had been a good mate, and we had already been through so much together. And young Ned, he was just a boy. Several other of our boys were killed, and our CO was beside himself with grief and anger. He made a formal complaint, but I don't know what came of it. What a waste. It's one thing to be killed in the line of duty by the enemy, but by your own allies? I can tell you those Yanks were cursed and reviled up and down the Regiment. If those Mitchells had returned we would probably have fired on them!

We stayed at L'Aigle for a few days to recuperate, and we were allocated a new crew member. His name was Wareham, and because he was such a huge bloke, we nicknamed him Bull. My little spell as tank commander came to an end when we got our new Sergeant, Jack Price. I had to show him the ropes as we went along, but I didn't mind, he soon fitted in with us and we became good mates. I went back to my original post as the gunner, and in a way I was glad to let Jack take some of the responsibility off of my shoulders. He hadn't been in action before, and he was very nervous at first, but we all gave him our support, and he turned out to be a very competent number one.

On 28 August we reached the River Seine at Rouvrey, and crossed by pontoon bridge that same evening. We were the first British artillery to cross the river.

Now, as I have said, we were an Armoured Mobile Brigade, and we had to be ready to move very quickly to anywhere that support was needed. After Falaise the Germans were on the run, but in some sections they were putting up a lot of resistance. They were holding on to an airfield just the far side of a town called Beauvais, and orders came through for us to join in the attack. We heard through the grapevine that our lads had pushed the Jerries out of the town, and as the British went through the locals cheered, and hung out the Union Jacks. Then the Jerries put in a counter-attack and pushed our blokes back again, so the Union Jacks disappeared and were replaced by the Swastikas!

When we reached Beauvais there was one hell of a battle going on. It raged for some time, but finally we put in a flanking movement from one side, and the Guards Armoured Division did the same on the opposite flank, and we soon had the Jerries surrounded. Hundreds of them surrendered, and our biggest prize was one of their generals. Quite a lot of them escaped, but we captured loads of equipment and several aircraft.

Later on our Regiment was to be awarded medals for the battle. Our Commanding Officer received the Distinguished Service Order, and there were three French Croix de Guerres. It seemed strange that one of these should be awarded to RSM Hector Bennett, because he didn't take part in the battle! He was at home in England on compassionate leave! There were twenty-four Military Crosses, twenty-four Military Medals, and twenty-four Mentioned in Dispatches. The Military Crosses all went to the officers of course, and the Military Medals went in the hat, but only for the rank of sergeant and above. The Mentions went in the hat for us other ranks, but I wasn't one of the lucky ones.

We carried on pursuing the fleeing Germans, but there wasn't much action to speak of. We went through places like Amiens and Arras, and started making our way towards Lille. When we reached there and drove through the town there were thousands of French people lining the streets. We were showered with flowers, and champagne was being drunk by the bucket. People clambered up over our vehicles and tanks, wanting to shake hands, and to kiss us. And some of those young French women weren't half bad! It made it very difficult to keep headway, but who can blame them? They had been living in fear and degradation and were just overjoyed to see us.

After we left Lille, we drove on for several miles, but suddenly we came under fire. The Germans had stopped running and had dug in. So, we wearily found ourselves back in battle. There was fierce fighting the whole of the next week, mainly long-range shelling and air attacks. We were strafed twice by a Messerschmitt 109, but he didn't do us a lot of damage. We tried to shoot him down, but he got away unscathed.

After this we were given another break, and we withdrew a couple of miles behind the lines. We were deployed in a big field, so we dug small trenches and ran the SPs over the top. This was necessary because we were still being shelled from long range. On the second day we were there, a mobile bath unit turned up, and we were able to have a shower. I can't tell you what a relief that was. We were filthy! The shower was just a long pipe sticking out from the back of a lorry. The water was barely warm, but to us it was real luxury. It was wonderful. We also got a change of underwear, and clean socks. My old ones stank to high heaven, when I took them off it looked as if I was wearing another pair underneath!

As I mentioned previously we were being continually shelled and bombarded, and trips to the latrine required extreme caution. One evening I needed to go to the toilet, and as it was peeing down with rain I put my gas cape over my head and made a dash for it. I said latrine. In reality all it consisted of was a trench that we had dug in the field next to the encampment. It was about a hundred yards from my bivouac. I reached the trench, straddled it, and squatted down. Before I could start what I went there for, I heard the sound of a shell coming over, and it exploded about two hundred feet in front of me. I didn't take too much notice, we were used to it by now, but then another shell dropped just behind me, and I thought, 'Blimey, they're ranging on me!' Then a salvo screamed by immediately overhead, and there was only one thing I could do. I jumped down the hole! Fortunately I was wearing a pair of gum boots at the time! After that first salvo had exploded I jumped out of the latrine and ran back towards my nice safe hidey-hole. Explosions seemed to pursue me all the way. I forced my way through a hedge and into a ditch on the other side which was full of stinging nettles. Then I scuttled back into our trench, and I was about as welcome as a skunk at a picnic!

When I looked at that hedge the next day, I was amazed that I had actually got through it. It looked nigh-on impenetrable! It was a hawthorn hedge, really dense, and full of big thorns. Funny thing was, I hadn't got a scratch on me. The ditch was full of tall, angry-looking nettles, but again, I hadn't been stung! I walked up and down the length of that hedge, but there was no sign of a gap, or even a disturbance where I had got through. Remarkable. It just goes to show what you can do when you are frightened to death!

We were bombarded all through that night, and I can tell you, it wasn't a pleasant experience. The Germans were using a type of shell called an air-burst, which would explode a hundred feet or so above us, and release hundreds of small grenades which would bounce about all over the place. You could never be sure where they would go off, and we reckoned that they had little legs and would run around until they found a slit-trench to jump into!

Another hazard of that type of continuous bombardment was the chance that you might get shell-shocked, or as we called it, 'bomb-happy'. Many boys did get bomb-happy, and believe me, it wasn't a pretty sight. On one occasion one of our blokes went completely off his rocker, and we actually had to sit on him all night to stop him from running away. The poor devil was screaming blue murder! When those kind of things happened we tried to keep our nerve by singing as loudly as we could! Mind you, it didn't seem to happen when we were in action; when we were firing back at the enemy, we didn't have time to be scared!

Anyway, back into action we went, and this time we pushed on up into Belgium. The Germans were fighting back like demons, and our advance came to a halt outside the town of Ghent. A ding-dong battle then ensued with a Jerry Panzer Division, and they were fiercely determined not to let us through. In one of the scraps that we had, three of their Tiger tanks attacked our position, and we soon found out how fanatical the SS troops could be. We knocked out two of the tanks, but the third kept coming straight at us with his guns blazing. Even when it became obvious that they were up against overwhelming odds they wouldn't surrender, and every last man of them was killed.

As the Germans retreated they left volunteer snipers behind, and one of our jobs was to flush them out. They would hide themselves in church towers, or up factory chimneys, any building that was tall. The way we dealt with them was to simply blast away at their hideouts. It always seemed rotten to me to have to line my sights onto a lovely old church tower and then to demolish it, but they had to be stopped. The German snipers were all sharpshooters, and they did a lot of damage. We always cheered when we saw one of the blighters tumble down from out of a tower, or off of a chimney.

After six weeks of continuous fighting we were once again taken out of action and given a rest. We stopped near Brussels and spent a few days in a convenient barracks. It was great to sleep in a proper bed for a change, and to eat food that we hadn't had to cook for ourselves.

One evening some of us were lucky enough to get passes to go into Brussels. We made for a hotel which had been converted into a huge NAAFI, and we were amused to see that it had been renamed 'Café Blighty'. We were able to have a shower, and while we were having our hair cut our uniforms and boots were taken away and cleaned. Later on that evening we went to a night club called 'Maxims', and some of the lads pestered me to go up on stage and sing. After a few beers I agreed, and went and asked the band leader if he knew 'Pennies from Heaven'. Anyway, they let me sing, and it went down a treat! We had a wonderful evening, and the war seemed a world away. Alas, it was all over too soon, and the next day it was back to the conflict.

Belgium was soon liberated, and so we pushed on up into Holland.

21

The Battle of the Bulge and Three Bridges

The fighting became even more savage, and our losses began to mount up. One of our talented young officers, Jimmy Savage [see Notes on the Text], was leading a reconnaissance patrol, and they were jumped on by a company of German paratroopers and completely wiped out. We came to the outskirts of Eindhoven and while we were there we were involved in a lot of street fighting. The Germans fought back bravely, but eventually they were beaten, and we finally drove in triumph through the centre of town. As with all the other towns and cities we had liberated, the local people lined the streets, and treated us like heroes.

It was now coming up to Christmas, and it was getting very cold. We were issued with aviators' flying suits, we called them Zoot-suits, they were kapok-filled and were very warm. While we were resting in Eindhoven the Regiment decided to put on a Christmas party for the local kids, and arrangements were made to hold it in a school hall on Christmas Eve. Everything was ready, and we were so looking forward to it, but then at noon-day of Christmas Eve we were told that we were going back into action.

Apparently, because the Germans were running short of fuel, they had started to advance on Liege back in Belgium, where the Allied petrol dumps were situated. In order to reach Liege they had to go through the Ardennes Forest which was being held by the Americans. The Yanks outnumbered the Jerries by at least five to one, but they couldn't hold them. It was imperative to prevent the Germans from getting through to our fuel dumps, if they had reached them it would have prolonged the war for months. So, we were sent down there to bolster up the Yanks. There were four divisions, the 50th, the 43rd, the Guards Armoured, and us, the 8th. The subsequent conflict became known as the Battle of the Bulge, and when we got there, we found that the Americans were being slaughtered.

As we went into action we saw hundreds and hundreds of dead American soldiers. Most of them had been stripped of their boots. The Yanks had been issued with these lovely brown half-length leather boots, and I suppose that the Jerries must have fancied them. Together we managed to push the enemy back, mostly because they were short of ammunition, food, and fuel. You had to realise that the German Army was an efficient, ruthless fighting machine. After prolonged fierce and bloody fighting they retreated, and the battle was over. To be fair, the Americans had fought back bravely, they just seemed to be very poorly organised. I wasn't much impressed by their officers, they seemed to me to be mainly death-or-glory boys, and the discipline was very poor. I heard later that they had lost forty thousand men in the battle, whereas our losses were less than a thousand.

So we returned to Eindhoven, and the local kids had a belated Christmas party. We had another much-needed break, and I remember being taken with a bunch of other lads on a guided tour of the Phillips electrical factory. We were shown how the Germans had used the factory for making their radar equipment etc, and how the Dutch people had been forced to work there for next to nothing.

The Allied advance had now reached something of a stalemate, and the enemy was holding fast. The Allied commanders then made one of their biggest mistakes, and came up with the doomed plan of an airborne attack on three bridges. These were situated at Grave, Nijmegen, and Arnhem. The idea was to get behind the Jerries and cut them off, but it didn't turn out quite as planned. The Yanks made the drop at Grave, and took the bridge with hardly any trouble at all. We soon reached them and consolidated the position, and then the same thing happened at the Nijmegen Bridge. The Yanks captured it, and again we pushed up to relieve them. The Yankee paratroopers were from the 105th Airborne Division, and they were nicknamed The Screaming Eagles. I must say that for Yanks they were damn good, they were the only American soldiers we came across that we had any confidence in!

However, we had to get across the Nijmegen Bridge and push on up to the British troops who were having a very tough time at Arnhem. The bridge was being continuously shelled, as well as being attacked from the air, and any vehicle attempting to cross it was liable to be blown up. We were instructed to go one at a time between salvos, but it was literally touch and go. While we were waiting for our turn Captain Warburton came over to speak to us, and he sounded just like Noel Coward in one of those war films. Very dramatically, he said, 'Well, there's nothing for it chaps, we just have to go on!' Anyway, our turn came, and Flash put his foot down and went like a bat out of hell. We had never seen the old girl go so fast, and we were mighty relieved when we reached the other side!

We carried on up the road towards Arnhem, but we came to a halt because the road was flooded. There are two rivers between Nijmegen and Arnhem, the Waal and the Maas [see General Richardson's notes on 'Operation Market Garden']. The bloody Germans had blown up the banks of both rivers, and they had been successful in flooding the whole area. The terrain on both sides of the road consisted of low-lying fields, so there was no possibility of driving around the floods. Progress was painfully slow, and was made even more difficult by the fact that we were being continually shelled by the German's long-range guns. The whole thing was becoming a real shambles. Eventually we found some dry ground where we could deploy our SPs so that we could have a go back at the enemy. Nonetheless, we were stuck there for days.

We had been a long time without changing our clothes or having a bath, and quite frankly, I was beginning to stink. Worse than that, I had begun to itch like mad. I put up with it for as long as I could, but finally I had to give in. I reported to the sick bay, and our medical officer showed me these horrible little creatures that were crawling under my skin. I thought to myself, 'Oh God, don't let it be crabs!' As it turned out it wasn't, but it was still something pretty unpleasant, it was scabies!

A bridge at Nijmegen, 1999. By Bill Davies.

The doctor sent me back to Nijmegen Hospital to be fumigated. What a performance! And how embarrassing! First of all I had to be shaved all over, including my head. Then I had to stand with my arms outstretched while a young nurse painted me all over with Blue Unction. All my clothes and my blankets were burned, and I was issued with new ones. It didn't clear up right away, and it was two more days before I was allowed to go back to the Regiment.

When I rejoined my crew, I found that the company was still pinned down by enemy bombardment, and we still couldn't move forward to relieve those poor devils at Arnhem. We were all frantic to get going, we all knew from the grapevine what was going on, and of course what happened there is now history. To say simply that they had a bad time wouldn't do them justice, those boys were literally in hell.

It looked as if we were going to be stuck in one place for some considerable time, so when I had a call from our Headquarters requesting that I take part in a concert there, I was damn pleased to get away for a while. I borrowed a bog-wheel (motor-bike to you) and drove off to Nijmegen. I won't dwell too much on the concert, suffice it to say that it was a huge success. I had two spots, in the first half I sang 'Danny Boy', and in the second I sang a popular song of that time called 'My Russian Rose'. It was great to bask in the limelight for a while, and I was treated to a slap-up meal and a few beers.

I set off back for the Regiment, but by this time it was very late and it was pitch dark. I was very tired, and before long I became totally lost. I drove down all these long winding country lanes, and as I was going down one that had tall hedges on either side, a shadowy figure stepped out into the road and challenged me. I nearly fell off the bike!

This chap was a sentry for an infantry company that was sheltering in the next field, and I explained to him where I had been, and that I was lost. He said, 'Well, I wouldn't carry on down road this mate if I was you, the Jerries are camped two hundred yards away!'

Feeling like a bit of a berk, I very quickly turned around and shot off the other way. I tried for the next hour to find my way back, but I really felt exhausted. Then I noticed a cottage with a barn next to it, so I decided to kip down there for the night and wait for day break. Just as I was about to settle down, an old man appeared, and after a lot of sign language, he led me into the cottage. His wife was a typical Dutch countrywoman, very jolly with rosy cheeks, and she made me a great big cheese sandwich and a warming cup of coffee. After that they showed me to a bed and said good night. Unfortunately the bed was full of bugs, and I didn't want to reawaken the scabies! So I crept out of the house and went back to the barn.

As soon as it was light I set off once again. I left the old couple a packet of cigarettes for their trouble. I only travelled another mile, and there was my Regiment. There was a lot of activity, it seemed that we were about to move out.

I decided to check all my belongings before we hit the road, and found to my consternation that I had lost a fifty guilder note. That's about five pounds in English money. I was scratching my head when I suddenly remembered while I had been in the barn the previous night I had had a call of nature. As a good soldier I had borrowed a spade and dug a hole in the adjacent field, and I remembered that in the pitch dark I had found a handy piece of paper in my pocket to use as toilet tissue. It had been the fifty guilder note!

My course of action was clear, I went and nabbed the motor-bike again, drove the mile back to the barn, went to the field, and dug up my money! It was a bit soiled, but that didn't stop me from spending it!

22

The Plönes Family

We never did get to Arnhem. By the time the first Allied troops reached the British boys there, they had just about been wiped out. We did see some of the survivors as they were making their way back, the poor devils looked just about all in. I will always remember the despair in their faces. I can still picture them; they were grey men, their uniforms were grey, their faces were grey, and most of them appeared to have grey hair. I often wondered about the old wives' tale that your hair can go grey overnight in times of stress or hardship.

By this time we were not meeting a lot of opposition, but the Jerries still had one or two tricks up their sleeves. Sabotage was the name of the game, aimed at doing as much damage to our forces as possible. Every road and bridge had to be checked, and our Engineers had a hell of a job keeping us on the move. Booby traps were everywhere, and we were told to be vigilant, but some of the troops got careless. I remember watching one soldier pick up a German helmet. He saw it lying at the edge of the road, and he ran over and picked it up, thinking that it would make a nice souvenir. What he didn't know was that it had been booby-trapped with a stick grenade. It blew up and the poor lad was killed.

We were now about due for another rest so we made our way back from the line. We went down through Eindhoven and on through Maastricht to a town called Heerlen, not far from the border with Germany. We stopped in an area of the town called Trebek. It was a pleasant residential area, a bit like an upmarket council estate. I was a bit surprised, because we had been told that there was a coal mine nearby. Among the troops, the area became known as 'Essex Village'.

There was a square in the middle of the estate, the centre of which was a small tree-lined green. We parked our tanks and vehicles around the square and then waited patiently as each crew was allocated a billet with a Dutch family. I went to a family named Plönes who lived at 13 Plataanstrasse. Now, what can I say about my lovely Plönes family? I only stayed with them for a little over a week,

Plataan Square, *c.*1945. From a postcard.

but their kindness touched my heart, and in that short period I became almost as close to them as to my own family.

Alfred and Greta were middle-aged, but their children were quite young, I guessed that they had married a little late in life. Daughter Betsjie was the oldest, she was about ten, her sister Crisjie was a couple of years younger, and Freddy was about six. They were beautiful blond kids, looking up at me with shy little smiles. Old Alfred had quite a slim figure, but Greta was a big buxom lady with sparkling blue eyes.

These wonderful people made me very welcome on that first night, and although none of us could speak the other's language, we got on like a house on fire. When I finally went to bed I was stuffed full of grub. I remember in particular a delicious apple strudel made by Greta. God alone knows where they got all the food from, because they were as poor as church mice. Nevertheless, it was quite a feast. I had a spotlessly clean bed to sleep in, and for the first time in months I enjoyed a full, uninterrupted night's sleep.

I woke early the next morning, having borrowed one of Alfred's shirts to sleep in. I looked around for my trousers, but they had vanished! So had everything else! I soon realised that all my clothes had been spirited away during the night. I

The Plönes family after the war. Courtesy of Mrs L. Davies.

Chris and Betsie, 1944. Courtesy of Mrs L. Davies.

looked out of the window, and there on the clothes line were all my clothes, my webbing equipment; even my kit-bag had been washed, and was hanging there to dry. I found Alfred's dressing gown and went downstairs to explain to Greta that I needed a uniform to go on parade with. The dear lady quickly pressed a pair of slacks and a blouse for me, and then I found that both of my black berets had been washed! While these were drying Alfred polished my boots and cleaned my brasses for me, so when I got on parade I must have been the cleanest and smartest soldier in the Army!

Some of the local people worked at the mine, but Alfred had been the manager of a shoe factory. Many of his neighbours had worked there under him. While the Germans were in occupation the factory was used to make munitions for them. The Dutch people were forced to work there for very low pay, in fact it was not far short of slave labour.

The family and I soon learned to understand each other, I was picking up a few words of Dutch, and they were picking up English very quickly. They spoke German very well, and I understood quite a lot of German words, so with all that, plus a little sign language, we got on famously. Greta and Alfred treated me like a long-lost son, in fact Greta insisted that she was my Dutch mother, and I had to call her Mum! The kids looked on me as a kind of big brother, and I used to sing to them, and play games with them. They wanted to know what rank I was, so I told them I was a Bombardier. They couldn't understand that, so I used the alternative title of Corporal. I told them that a soldier with one stripe was a Lance Corporal, or 'little' Corporal, and that my two stripes meant that I was a full Corporal, or 'big' Corporal. They latched on to that, and for the rest of my stay with them I was known as 'Der Grosse Caporal' or 'Corporal Ronnie'.

All the Dutch families had more or less been living on a starvation diet for ages. It was wonderful to see their faces when we gave them some of our rations, they hadn't seen decent food for years. We were all getting pretty good at communicating with each other, and we used to sit around after our evening meal swapping stories. We told them about our families, and life in England. We also told them about the invasion and all the action we had seen so far. In return, they told us about life under the Nazi yoke!

Alfred told us how the Mayor of Heerlen had fallen out of favour with the District Gauleiter, and had consequently been paraded around the streets in disgrace wearing a dog collar and lead. They even made him walk on all fours. We were appalled to find out how terrible it had been for the Dutch Jews. They had been beaten and humiliated, and made to wear a conspicuous Jewish emblem. Finally they had all been rounded up and transported to concentration

Chris, Betsie and Freddy, *c.*1944. Courtesy of Mrs L. Davies.

camps. Many of these poor souls had been friends and neighbours of Alfred and Greta, and most of them were never seen again.

Another story was how after the liberation all the local women who had collaborated by fraternising with the German soldiers had been punished in front of jeering crowds by having all their hair cut off.

Our days in Trebek were spent in replenishing our stores and ammunition, and cleaning and checking all our guns and equipment. However, we had plenty of free time. There were impromptu football matches on the green with the local people, and we organised all sorts of games and entertainment for the kids. One day we happened to drive our SP down Plataanstrasse, and just for a lark I swung it round so that the big gun was pointing straight at Greta's kitchen window, where she was busy working. It gave her the fright of her life! (When I spoke to Betsjie many years later, she told me that this was one of her most vivid childhood memories. Naughty Corporal Ronnie!)

As I mentioned earlier, we were only in Trebek for a little over a week, but we were so relaxed and happy, it seemed much longer. The family and I got to know each other really well. Greta asked all about my family, and I gave her several photos. She gave me photos of herself and Alfred, and the children, and I have always treasured them. I have them to this day.

The time came at last when we had to leave, and on that last night we had a little farewell party. We managed to get hold of a few bottles of British beer, and a bottle of Scotch. We stayed up until the early hours, toasting each other's health. The next morning we said our goodbyes, and everyone was in tears. We had exchanged addresses, and vowed to write to each other after the war. I'm glad to say that we did, we exchanged letters and photographs for many years, and finally Lily and I travelled to Holland in 1999 with my son and daughter-

Plönes children. Courtesy of
Mrs L. Davies.

Januari 5 1945

Mrs Davies

I introduce me, alls the seconds
mother from Ronny. You housebant.
He is our best friends He came two
times when holiday to my home
And he is here like son in house.
He say alltimes to me, you is me
seconds mammy, me mammy in Holland
My three children they like him, like
her own father And Ronny he like
my boys almost so much alls his own
boys. Mrs Davies when I may
Will you send me an foto from you
boys plees? That makes our happyly
The foto from you merrid stay be our
in the room, on the best plaes. And the
foto from Ronny in Billy too.
When Ronny come in the first time
he shew it me befor then minuts

Left: The first page of Greta's original
letter, dated 5 January 1945. Courtesy of
Mrs L. Davies.

Below: Chris Plönes with Ron and Lily,
1999. By Bill Davies.

Ron outside 13 Plataanstrasse, 1999. By Bill Davies.

in-law, to see Chrisje and Betsjie, and Betsjie's husband Franz. Sadly, by that time dear Greta and Alfred had passed away, and so had Freddy.

We drove out of Heerlen and headed for the German border. This was a very significant point in the campaign, and was a huge boost to our troops' morale. As we crossed into Deutschland there was a huge cheer from the lads, it was a very exciting moment.

The first German town of any size that we came to was Geilenkirchen, and you won't be surprised when I tell you that this time there was no cheering from the locals. What we did see was hundreds of refugees streaming out of town. We found a big warehouse full of provisions. There were hams, sides of bacon, bags of sugar and flour, boxes of butter, loads of tinned fruit, and a lot more besides. We discovered that all this food was being stored for the German officers and high-ranking civilians, not for the ordinary soldiers, and certainly not for the townspeople. We felt quite justified in confiscating a fair bit of it, but rest assured, we didn't keep it all of for ourselves.

We divided it up so that each crew got a fair amount of grub, and the rest was packed up in boxes, and labelled with the names and addresses of our Dutch friends in Trebek. When our supply trucks came up the next day we asked them to deliver them for us, and I am glad to say they did. We did this on a couple of occasions, and we also found a clothing depot, and sorted out decent coats, suits, shoes, and all sorts of dresses which were also sent back down the line to our friends.

Chris Plönes with Alfred. Courtesy of Mrs L. Davies.

23

Beyond The Siegfried Line

One of our tasks was to destroy the local banks. We were also instructed to burn all the money. We had a very exciting time blowing open all the steel security doors, and setting explosives to blast into the vaults. There were stacks and stacks of banknotes, they were in all kinds of denominations; you can imagine our feelings when we saw all that lovely money and then had to burn it. Of course, being human we were tempted to pocket some of it, but we weren't bright enough to work out which would be the best notes to keep. I picked up a couple of large notes, one for seven million deutschemarks, and another one for six million. I thought that when the war was over, I would be rich! Of course, I couldn't have been more wrong, after the war only banknotes up to ten marks were declared legal; anything above that was worthless. I haven't any idea how many small denomination notes we burned, but there we were, throwing the wrong ones on the bonfire! There must have been millions going up in smoke. What a twit I was!

We left Geilenkirchen and pushed on towards the River Rhine, but we had to cross the Siegfried Line first. From what we had learned about the German Army, we thought that we would be hard pressed to get across it. To our great surprise, we met with very little resistance, in fact it was a piece of cake. The Jerries had completely scarpered and so we just sailed through. No trouble at all. I'll give you three guesses what we were singing! It was quite an impressive sight, there were Dragon's Teeth all over the place, designed to hinder armoured vehicles. They were wicked-looking pointed concrete stakes placed in the ground at an angle. There were various other types of tank-traps, but our Engineers had cleared the way. We also saw huge pill-boxes, and vast underground passages, I wasn't sure what they were for, but I guessed that that was where the top German Brass had their quarters.

The German Army was now in full retreat, we had definitely got them on the run. We chased them for miles, but before we got to the Rhine, they turned and made a stand. We made it to a town called Goch, and it was decided that we would rest there for a couple of nights. There wasn't much of the town left, it had been virtually razed to the ground, the buildings had all been destroyed by aerial bombardment. The German artillery was shelling us heavily, so we needed to find shelter, and we decided that the safest place was underground.

There were hundreds of cellars to choose from, so we found ourselves a nice big dry one, and settled down. There was no door to the cellar so we just put a blanket across the opening to keep out the draught. The blokes were getting hungry, and as it was my turn to cook, I set about preparing our evening meal.

After we had been there for about half an hour we were beginning to get quite comfortable. Food was cooking, one or two of the blokes had started to strip down and clean their small-arms, and Flash had just stretched out on his bed-roll. Suddenly, the blanket across the opening was violently pulled back, and I kid you not, there in the doorway stood the biggest and meanest looking storm-trooper I had ever seen. From where I was standing he looked at least ten feet tall! To my horror, I saw that he was holding a machine gun, which he was pointing straight at me! Well I can tell you, I nearly soiled my pants, I really thought my last moment had come.

You never saw such a scramble in all your life, blokes were leaping to their feet, frantically trying to re-assemble their weapons. To be completely honest, I just stood there with my mouth open. Then this demon in German uniform threw the gun down, raised his arms, and shouted 'Kamerad!'

We followed him out of the cellar, and there on the road outside was a whole company of German soldiers. By this time the rest of our lads, who were occupying other cellars, had turned out, and the Germans surrendered their weapons. We sat them down in the road with their hands on their heads, and before long the Military Police came along and marched them away.

Well, it certainly gave us a scare, but it wasn't the only one we got that night! Worse was to follow. We went back down into the cellar, settled down again, and I served up the grub. After a while we turned in for what we thought was going to be a good night's sleep. At around two in the morning we all woke up. The air in the cellar seemed to be lifting somehow, and there was this horrible high-pitched sound. We switched on our torches, and what seemed to be thousands of little eyes were lit up, we had been overrun with rats! They were all over us, in our clothes, all over the food, they seemed to be in a frenzy. I have never been so scared in all my life, and that includes the storm-trooper!

We ran out of that cellar as if the Devil himself was after us! We searched the area for another cellar, but they were all occupied. Our only available shelter from the bombardment was our old rat-infested cellar, but we couldn't face that again, so we decided to sleep out in the open under the SP, and take a chance on being blown up. The next morning as we chatted to some of the other blokes, we found out that many other crews had suffered the same experience. One wag joked that as we were fairly close to Hamelin, we should have gone looking for the Pied Piper!

We drove on, deeper into Germany, and after a couple of days we caught our first glimpse of the River Rhine. There it was, stretched out in front of us. We were coming down out of the surrounding hills, so we were looking down on it. It was a beautiful sight. It looked so peaceful that it was hard to believe that there was a war going on. The river was quite wide at this point, and we heard that the Engineers were going to build a Bailey bridge. Well, they did their best, but the enemy were shelling the river very heavily. This held up the advance for quite a time. The problem was, our side of the river was more or less open fields, whereas the enemy side was thickly wooded, giving them the advantage. The Allies set up a huge artillery barrage which was code-named 'Operation Veritable' to clear the way for us to cross.

One of the things I remember was all the dead fish floating on top of the water. Hundreds of them, and they didn't half stink! The Royal Engineers tried to build a pontoon bridge across the river but it was suicide, they lost so many men that the operation had to be called off.

All the tank crews were called together for a briefing, and we were told that we would be crossing by raft. During the night the Engineers and a force of Commandos went across the river in rubber dinghies, covered by a huge artillery barrage from our side. The noise was terrific, ear-shattering. Once they had got across they pulled across more dinghies filled with equipment, and set about erecting big donkey engines to tow the rafts across.

Just as dawn was breaking a squadron of Allied planes flew very low along the river and laid down a smoke screen. It was dense, acrid smoke, everyone had to wrap scarves around their faces to stop themselves from choking. We made our way down to the river bank and loaded our SPs onto these huge rafts; the SPs were then secured with big chains.

Next came that horrible journey on our raft. The water was rough and very choppy, I thought that we would capsize at any moment. The bombardment was intense, shells were exploding all around us. Some of the rafts were hit, throwing men and tanks into the river. There were lots of blokes struggling in the water, but our orders were explicit, we were not to stop for any reason whatsoever. So we couldn't help them, it was very frustrating.

At the time the whole business seemed utterly chaotic, but in reality it was very well-organised. By the time we had driven off the raft onto dry land the Allied infantry and the Commandos had established a secure bridgehead, and before long we had set up and joined in the British artillery attack.

24

Watch Out For Thunderbolts!

All that day we fired our guns, until in the finish they became red hot, so we had to stop and let them cool down. Then we started to advance. At first progress was slow, and we only gained a few miles. By the next day the enemy had started to withdraw, and were once more on the run. It was clear that the Germans had started to get desperate, and this was illustrated by the fact that the prisoners we were taking were either very young or very old. Mind you, some of them were still pretty arrogant. The famous Luftwaffe were rarely seen by this time, but we did have a few anxious moments. The Browning point five machine gun mounted on our hull was put to good use during a number of isolated air attacks, in fact we claimed a hit on one Messerschmitt 109. It crashed in some trees just behind us, but we never found out for sure if it was us who had shot it down.

We pushed further into Germany, bypassing Cologne and Dusseldorf, and came at last to a halt in the Reichwald Forest. It was huge, twice as big as Epping Forest, and the trees were mainly pine, which made it very difficult to work in. We were constantly under shellfire, and the danger came not only from shrapnel, but also from falling trees. When a shell hit one of the trees pieces of it would fly in all directions, and in fact a lot of our boys were wounded with damn great lumps of wood sticking out of them.

One day we came to an open stretch of countryside and on the far side there was a wooded area. The Jerries had set up a big gun in there which was doing untold damage. Our Group had been given the task of destroying it, but it was well defended, and we were having a rough time of it. In these situations our Commanding Officer established direct radio contact with whoever was providing our air cover, directing aerial attack onto the target. Sometimes it would be the RAF, mainly flying Typhoons, and at other times it would be the American Air Force with Thunderbolts. On this particular day it was the Yanks, and the CO called for a 'Stonk' as we called it, on the enemy position.

The Thunderbolts suddenly appeared overhead, and circled round us. There were six of them, and they were a welcome sight as they peeled off behind us. We cheered them on as they released their deadly rockets; we felt perfectly safe after having set up our recognition markers and smoke-pots. To our horror, as the rockets came screaming down, we saw that they were aiming at us instead of the Germans! All six planes had a go at us, despite the fact that we were sending up yellow smoke, which was the standard recognition signal. It was as clear as crystal that we were on their side, but even so, after the rocket attack they circled round and flew in very low to strafe us with machine gun fire. The Jerries must have thought it was their birthday, they intensified their bombardment, and we suffered terrible losses.

Twenty-four men were killed in that attack, and several more were wounded. They also destroyed some of our SPs. I can honestly say that on that occasion we hated the Yanks every bit as much as the Germans! You accept the danger of being killed by the enemy, but to be killed by your own side is unforgivable. I never did find out what happened about it, I know our CO was absolutely livid, so I'm sure he kicked up a stink. We were so badly mauled that we had to be withdrawn from the action. We retreated two miles down the line to what we thought was a safe area. There we rested, and tried to repair some of the damage, but it seemed that the Yanks still hadn't finished with us!

One evening we had just sat down to have some grub when a shell screamed over our heads and burst in the trees behind us. This was rapidly followed by another which came straight at us and only just missed. We took post in our SP, and I swung our gun in the direction that the shells had come from. I fully expected to see a German tank, but when I looked through my sights I saw that it was a Yankee! He was still firing at us, despite the unmistakable white star painted on our sides. We had no idea why he was attacking us, but Captain Sidgewick said to put a round over his head which I did, and the stupid bugger shot off.

To add insult to injury, we had yet another Yankee experience that night. There were a load of German prisoners of war near us being guarded by some Pioneer Corps blokes, and a platoon of American soldiers appeared, and stumbled into them. They must have thought they had run into the German Army, because the leader of the platoon stuck his hands up in the air and shouted out 'Kamerad!' The rest of the platoon followed suit, and you should have heard the jeers from our blokes! The air was ripe, I can tell you! When the Yanks realised their mistake they slunk off with their tails between their legs, and our blokes were booing and shouting insults at them.

After these incidents we didn't have much time for the Yanks, we didn't think much of them at all. It was obvious to us that their army was very poorly trained, and lacking in discipline. Right up until the end of the war I saw nothing to change my opinion of them. The only exception, as I have mentioned previously, was the Screaming Eagles. I get very impatient when I see films depicting all American soldiers as heroes, and winning the war without our help, it is all a load of crap.

We were still resting when the news came that the first leave passes were about to be issued. I was delighted when I found out that my name was in the second batch of names to go. Just imagine the excitement among the troops, after all the shelling, and bombing, and being shot at, we were getting a chance to go home! When my turn came, I made damn sure that I was going to be safe! The evening before we were due to go, I got ready, washed and dressed, put my greatcoat on and went outside. I sat on the edge of a fox-hole all night, ready to jump in if anything happened. In the morning a truck came to pick us up, and me and the rest of the blokes who were shipping out jumped in quickly. We urged the driver to shove off, before we came under attack.

It had rained all through the night, and it was very muddy in the forest. We had only gone a couple of hundred yards down the bridle path, when the truck became stuck in the mud! To a man, and without being told, which is unusual for a soldier, we jumped out and pushed and shoved that truck, if we had had to we would have pushed it all the way home! We finally got it moving, and before long we got onto a main road, and after a long, long journey, we arrived at Calais. We got on a boat, and after an uneventful crossing, we arrived at Dover. I caught a train to Victoria, and walked out of the station to catch a bus.

It felt kind of strange, with all the ordinary things going on around me. Buses! Queues! I sort of felt that people would give three cheers or something, I felt as if I had 'D-Day' written all over my chest. I just stood there for a few minutes, but then I realised that no one was taking any notice of me. The only consolation that I had was the fact that the conductor wouldn't take my fare.

The bus took me to Liverpool Street, and then there was the familiar journey to Brimsdown Station. When I walked into Jack's Newsagents in Brimsdown Avenue for a packet of fags, the war seemed a million miles away. I hadn't seen my darling Lily since that night I had jumped ship in Southampton harbour, and it was wonderful to take her in my arms again. It was just marvellous to be with her, and our lovely sons. They were growing up fast, and I thought, 'Hang on! I'm missing out on something here!' Billy was nearly five, Steve was three, and little Michael was eighteen months. I can still picture Billy and Steve looking up at me, spellbound, as I told them some of my adventures. We made the most of that week, it was lovely being home, but all the time a little voice inside me was saying, 'Don't go back mate!' We both knew that I might not be coming home ever again. I played with the boys, and bathed them, put them to bed, and told them stories, including some edited versions of some of my experiences in the Army, as well as all the other usual 'Daddy' things. Michael was a bit wary of me at first, but it didn't last long.

Poor Lily cried herself to sleep more than once that week. Then the crunch came when it was time to go back. I worried for her, too, and the boys. In the relative calm of home life I had time to realise that our wives were having a pretty rough time of it, what with the air-raids, the food rationing, and bringing up the kids in spite of all the hardships. I think that they deserved as many medals as the troops!

One of our biggest concerns when we were abroad was the thought of those horrible bombs and rockets being dropped on our loved ones. And the Doodle-bugs! I still remember that awful droning noise! Such horrors for defenceless women and children. I personally knew a few mates whose families had been killed in air-raids, and they were devastated. A lot of the boys went on leave to find their homes gone, and their families gone. One bloke in particular that this happened to came back off leave, and after brooding for a couple of days he shot himself. Poor soul. What a tragedy! So, you can understand why I didn't want to go back. But, like the good little soldier boy that I was, I said a very tearful goodbye to Lily and our children, and went back to the war.

25

Behind Enemy Lines

So off I went, back to Germany, via the same route. As we approached the battle area, my tummy turned over, and I wanted to go back home. But I didn't, when we got back I acted like a hero and ran straight into the nearest fox-hole! The Regiment hadn't moved an inch while I had been away, and there was one hell of a battle going on. I didn't even have time to change into my battle-dress, I was just put back into action within an hour of arriving. In at the deep end you might say.

It was shortly after this that I got sent on a couple of Jock Columns. Let me explain. A Colonel Jock Campbell, who was operating in the Middle-East War, had dreamed up a strategy where the infantry would put in an attack on the enemy front line and create a gap in their defences. Then, under the cover of darkness, an armoured column such as ours would shoot through the gap and swan off up the road, sometimes penetrating five or six miles behind enemy lines. The column would then stop at a site overlooking the road, camouflage themselves, and wait until morning.

When it became light the enemy supply trucks and vehicles carrying reinforcements would come rolling down the road, and would then come under attack. When sufficient damage had been done, the column would scarper, and it would be every man for himself until they got back to their own lines. The strategy was named after the bloke who dreamed it up!

Anyway, I went on a couple of these jaunts, and on one occasion we were on the edge of a wood overlooking a road, when sure enough, as dawn rose, a huge column of German trucks came in sight. As soon as they were level with us we opened fire, and we knocked hell out of them! Then we got the order to withdraw, so we turned and drove off. We went across country, hell for leather as we headed for our lines. At first we were going along OK, but gradually we started to get left behind. We shouted at Flash put his foot down, but after a while it dawned on us that there was something wrong with our engine! We got slower and slower, and before long we realised that we were not going to make it.

The rest of the column was long gone, and we started to get desperate, it looked as if we were completely on our own, behind enemy lines! Then we spotted a farm that had a Dutch barn, and Flash nursed our SP into it. We were only just in time, because as soon as Flash took his foot off the throttle, the engine cut out altogether. We were still dangerously close to a road, and we didn't want to be spotted, so we found a load of hay and camouflaged the SP to look like a hayrick. We didn't dare to light a fire, so it was cold grub for the rest of that day.

We couldn't even have a fag with all that hay about, and some of the lads started to get a bit edgy. When it started to get dark Jack sent me and Bull Wareham out on a recce to see what we could find. We were still wearing our Zoot suits, because it was very cold. We must have looked like beings from another planet! We were also well armed; I had an American Colt forty-five slung in a holster around my waist, and a Smith and Wesson thirty-eight strapped to my leg. Bull was also wearing his thirty-eight around his waist. Talk about cowboys! We crept along the road, and before long we heard the cackle of chickens, and then we came across a small stone cottage with a large garden.

As we were looking around to see what we could scrounge, the door of the cottage opened, and there stood a little old lady. She had a crutch under one arm, and we realised she only had one leg. She was holding up a hurricane lamp and peering at us, and then she smiled and gestured for us to come inside. She was very friendly, and soon we were both holding a steaming mug of coffee. In a mixture of German and English she told us that she was not German, she was Polish. She said that her husband was a farmer, and that they had been transported from Poland to work this farm for the Germans. Unfortunately he had been taken ill and had died, and she had buried him in the back garden. She also told us that there were many more Polish people in the district, but she said that they hated the Germans, and would not give us away.

She made some thick cheese sandwiches with home-made bread, and a big jug of coffee for the rest of the lads, and we went back to the SP. Before we left we promised her that we would come back the next night, that is if we were still there, and bring her some chocolate and some soap, which apparently she hadn't seen for years.

We stayed under cover all the next day and took it in turns to keep a look-out. When it was my turn I saw a German motor-bike and sidecar driving down the road. The bloke in the sidecar had a machine gun. I alerted the others, but they went straight past. Fortunately they were the only Jerries we saw while we were there. I should point out that our radio was also out of action, so we couldn't let our Regiment know where we were or what had happened to us.

That evening we went back to the Polish lady's cottage, and took some of our grub and some goodies with us. She was delighted with all this, and she cooked the grub for us, it made a wonderful meal. We chatted to the lady as best we could, she enjoyed hearing about Lily and my little boys, and I showed her the couple of photographs that I had in my wallet. It was a pleasant evening, but by the next day we were all getting anxious. We thought that surely our troops must have advanced by now, and what if our Regiment had advanced and gone around us? Blimey, we thought, we could be here for the duration!

After four days our grub ran out, and worse than that, our fags ran out! We had to rely on the old lady to feed us, but she was very good about it, and we certainly didn't starve! It was simple fare, but there was plenty of it. We just had to mooch about, mostly playing cards, and then on the fifth day we spotted a British jeep approaching us. We flagged it down, and it turned out to be a British infantry officer. He told us that our troops had made a breakthrough a couple of days before, and were already five miles ahead of us. We told him about the SP and he drove off, promising to report our position.

Later that day a recovery team turned up with a spare SP, so we transferred all our gear, supplies and equipment into it, and went to the cottage to say goodbye to that kind old Polish lady. We left the recovery team to deal with our crocked SP, and set off with directions to find the Regiment. We never did find out why the old girl (the SP that is!) had conked out, and we never got her back.

26

Belsen

It caused quite a stir when we got back, and we were told that if we hadn't got back when we did, we would have been posted as missing. All our mates were glad to see us, they had more or less given us up for lost.

By this time the Germans had been well and truly beaten, and were in full retreat. We pursued them, driving down one of the Autobahns for mile after mile, and we encountered little or no opposition. We finally stopped at a small town just short of Osnabruck, and while we were there we liberated one of the German's slave labour camps.

The inmates were mostly Russian prisoners of war, and I remember how dirty and emaciated they were. They looked as if they had had a very bad time of it. They cheered and sang when we arrived because they were so pleased to see us! We fed them, and gave them some decent clothes to wear, and then handed over the camp to our Welfare people.

We then bivouacked in a nearby field, and organised a meal for ourselves, and finally settled down for a good night's sleep. I hadn't been asleep for long when I was woken up and told to take a patrol into the town. The Russians had been set free, and gangs of them were roaming around bumping off local people, including women and children. It took us all night to round them up, and we had to take them back to the camp and lock them up. They vehemently hated all Germans, and couldn't understand why they couldn't be allowed to kill civilians. In fact they became furious with us for preventing them from doing so! We finally left them in the custody of the Military Police, and snatched a couple of hours of kip.

The next morning we were off again. We went on pursuing the same German troops, but the Yanks veered off to the east in the direction of the River Elbe and Berlin. It seemed that the American High Command wanted to pull off a propaganda coup by being the first of the Allied armies to reach Berlin. As we all know the Russians beat them to it, but that was their intention.

We carried on northwards towards the Baltic coast until we came to a town called Neustadt. It was a beautiful place, virtually untouched by Allied bombing. It was set in a lovely alpine valley, nestling at the foot of the Hartz Mountains. A river ran through the centre of the town, and you could see it cascading down the mountainside in a series of waterfalls. We came to a bridge, and the convoy got held up there, so we watched some of the local people catching salmon. There was a waterfall just above the bridge, and the fish were being caught as they leapt up it. Various methods were being used, mostly gaffes and nets, and it all looked so easy. We started to chat to some of these people, and guess what? It was fresh salmon for dinner!

We stayed there overnight, and continued on our way the next day. In just a few hours we reached the next town, which was called Celle. As we approached it we became aware of a horrible smell, it seemed to be everywhere. It was so bad you could almost touch it, a pervasive pong that got into everything, you just couldn't get away from it. When we had first entered the town we had caught a glimpse of what looked like a factory chimney in the distance, and we assumed that the smell was coming from there. We thought that perhaps it was a soap factory, or some kind of chemical plant. Whatever it was, the smell was so bad, it was putting us off our food. We observed that the chimney was still belching out great plumes of black smoke, and the smell seemed to increase in intensity. Some of the blokes were starting to feel sick, so we asked one of our officers if anything could be done about it. He gave us an odd look, and told us that what we were looking at was the infamous concentration camp of Belsen.

Of course, at this time we hadn't heard very much about these camps or the full extent of the persecution of the Jewish people, but we were soon to find out. When our B-Echelon group caught up with us, the cooks were told to fill hot-boxes with soup, and the Quartermaster had to provide a supply of blankets. A couple of dozen of us were selected to go to the camp to help our Welfare Staff to feed the poor unfortunate inmates. We had already begun to feel somewhat uneasy, and were under no illusion about the unpleasant aspects of our task. However, nothing, repeat nothing could have prepared us for the full horror of what we saw, heard, and smelled. As we got closer to Belsen the stench became literally unbearable, and we all had to tie scarves around our faces.

As we drove through the gates, we could see for ourselves the stark reality. I don't want to go into any more detail here, for one thing it distresses me trying to recall it, and for another I guess that there have been enough films and books about it for most people to know what was going on. What I will tell you is just how we all felt at the time. It made us sick to think just how any human being could treat their fellow men and women in such a vile way. We didn't see the worst, we weren't allowed to, but what we did see was enough. Our hatred of the Nazis increased a hundred-fold that day, and our fervent wish was that all the guilty would be brought to justice.

We fed all those who were still able to walk, and many of them had no concept of who we were. I'm pretty sure that some of them thought that it was the Germans who were feeding them. It was sometimes difficult to tell which were men and which were women, they all had shaved heads, and all were wearing those awful striped, pyjamas. There wasn't a smile anywhere, but there were an abundance of tears, and believe me they weren't all coming from the poor souls wearing stripes.

After we had finished helping to feed and comfort the prisoners, we had to go and pick up some of the camp guards who had been locked up in the Guard Room. It surprised me to see that many of them were women. Most of the men were very servile, they were terrified of us. I think that they thought we were going to shoot them, which quite frankly we felt like doing. The women however weren't like that at all, they were arrogant bitches, all of them. One in particular kept on sneering at us, and giving the Nazi salute. I felt like smashing her face in with my rifle butt, but we were better disciplined than that. We had full confidence in British justice, and knew that these evil people would get their just deserts. We escorted them back to Celle, and it was with considerable relief that we got rid of them.

We stayed in Celle for one week, and we spent most of that time hunting Nazis. I went out on a number of patrols, and following various tip-offs from Intelligence we searched some of the local houses. You should have seen some of those big houses, it was a real eye-opener to see how well the German elite lived. Many of them were filled with beautiful antique furniture, sumptuous decorations and fittings, and what looked like valuable paintings. In several instances we found cellars full of champagne and cases of whisky, how they came by them is anybody's guess, but I don't think it was for services to humanity! We picked up quite a few suspected Nazis, and in every instance they denied any connection to the Nazi Party. Despite their protests, we found plenty of evidence to prove them liars, some of it hidden away in concealed rooms. We found Nazi regalia and flags, photos and papers, and sometimes full Nazi uniforms. Once we had proof they were arrested and taken away for interrogation.

The thing that amazed all of us was that you could talk to any German in Celle, even the ordinary person on the street, and they would deny all knowledge of the activities of the Nazi Party, or of Belsen, even though it was just a couple miles down the road. It was as if the knowledge was too terrible to own, and that somehow they had collectively erased it from their memories. I was never more relieved than when we left that place.

27

The War is Over!

After leaving Celle, we pushed on towards Bremerhaven. It was now spring, and it was clear that the Germans couldn't hold out much longer. However, it seemed that they still had one or two tricks up their sleeves. As I have mentioned, the dreaded Luftwaffe was by now virtually non-existent, so it came as a bit of a surprise when we caught our first sight of their latest secret weapon.

One day, as we were approaching Bremerhaven, we heard a sound like a shell going over, so we all ducked for cover. Suddenly, a strange-looking plane screamed over, it was our first sight of a jet plane! We found out later that it was a Messerschmitt ME 262. It was a squat, ugly looking thing, but boy, did it go fast! He circled round and had a go at us, and we fired back, but he was going too fast to get a proper shot at him. Give the Germans their due, they weren't going to give in easily!

Mind you, we were seeing plenty of indications that the German troops were now completely demoralised. As we drove along the road we saw literally thousands of prisoners marching along in the opposite direction. Most of them didn't even have an escort. They moved slowly, heads down, most of them a picture of dejection and misery. You could see from the look on their faces that they were a beaten people.

We finally reached Bremerhaven, and almost immediately we became involved in fierce street-to-street fighting. There were sharpshooting German snipers everywhere, picking off Allied troops, but one by one we ferreted them out. The Germans had also left loads of booby traps around, and we spent a lot of time dismantling them. After a few days the fighting was finally over, and the town was under our control.

We were all beginning to get excited, we could almost smell victory. Rumours were rife, and we were hearing stories about all the top-ranking Nazis. One of the things we heard was that Himmler had been captured in the town harbour disguised as an ordinary sailor. It wasn't true, but it was a fact that many Nazis did disguise themselves as sailors in order to get on board ships and boats to get out of the country.

Word came down that an SS Panzer Regiment was holed up at Schleswig-Holstein on the Baltic coast, so that became our next objective. Our task was to sort them out, but they were not going to give in easily. We pushed them back, inch by inch, and as they retreated they blew great holes in the road to impede our progress. Luckily our Engineers had the service of bridge-laying tanks, and these were kept pretty busy. Those Panzer boys were damn good fighters, and despite what was by now more or less overwhelming odds, they were putting up a fierce struggle.

As we approached a small village one day, we went round a bend in the road, and were confronted by a bloody great Tiger tank. We were caught completely on the hop, and the fact that we were in convoy made us more vulnerable. He opened fire, and we sustained considerable damage. Our CO was in a Sherman tank at the head of the convoy and it was badly knocked about. He survived, but two of his crew were killed.

The Tiger just sat there blasting away, and eventually we outflanked him and finished him off, killing the whole crew. This was only one of dozens of similar scenarios, and it became clear that many of the more fanatic German soldiers, particularly the SS, were happy to fight to the death as long as they could take a few Allied troops along with them. We certainly lost a lot of our blokes in this kind of dogfight.

After much fierce fighting we arrived at Flensburg, which is the most northerly town in Germany, right up on the Danish border. It was while we were there that we heard that Hitler was dead, and that the German Army had surrendered on 2 May. I thought, 'Blimey, I wish that someone would tell this bunch of fanatics that are still giving us a hard time!'

We were beginning to get British newspapers now, although they were all a few days old, and you can imagine our feelings when we read that there had been a 'Victory in Europe' day celebrated all over Britain on 8 May! They were celebrating victory, but we were still losing blokes! We were very gradually winning the fight, flushing out the last dregs of the SS fanatics, despite the stiff resistance they were putting up. We pursued them all along the Baltic coast, right up to the harbour town of Kiel.

Then, out of the blue, came the day when I knew that the war was finally, indisputably over. You've heard me talk about barrages, artillery fire, aerial bombardment, mortar fire, machine gun and rifle fire etc etc etc. These are the unavoidable companions of war, and had been a part of our lives since that day the previous June. We didn't notice the noise after a while, it just became as naturally accepted as eating, breathing, and swatting flies. You could even sleep through it.

On this particular day we were having a break in the middle of a wood, and I suddenly became aware that I could hear voices. Then I realised that these voices were coming from beyond the clearing where we were sitting, and that the people I was hearing were not shouting. The guns had stopped! It was quiet, and it felt strange, uncanny, we had forgotten what quiet sounded like. I could even hear birds singing! I looked around me, and I saw blokes laughing and crying, and one or two had fallen to their knees and put their hands together in prayer.

Further up the line we heard cheers going up, and one of our officers came running up to us. He was so emotional he could hardly speak at first, but he finally got it out, and shouted, 'It's all over! The bloody war is over!' Well, we just went mad. There were men running about like loonies, jumping up in the air, flinging their arms around each other and dancing around, and punching the air in triumph. I wasn't one of those. I just sat down on the ground and cried with relief. What a wonderful moment that was. Bottles of Scotch whisky appeared, seemingly out of nowhere, and we drank a toast to each other out of our battered old tin mugs. The padre then asked all of us to kneel down on the grass and give thanks to God for the fact that we were still alive.

So, that was that, the war was over, and there was no more fighting to do. Nonetheless, there was still a hell of a lot of work to be done, and we were now an army of occupation.

B Troop at Maastricht, November 1944. Courtesy of the Essex Yeomanry.

28

Post-war Germany

We drove triumphantly into Kiel, and this time, some of the locals did actually cheer us! You could see the weariness of defeat on their faces, and most of them looked undernourished, in fact some of the kids looked half starved. Kiel is a naval base, it reminded me very much of Portsmouth, and in the harbour we could see lots of warships at anchor. Prominent among them was a huge great liner, it was an American ship, the *Milwaukee*. It had been captured by the Germans earlier on in the war, and the German High Command had been using it as their headquarters. As soon as the German officers had been escorted off, our High Command took it over for the same purpose.

We were taken to a large naval barracks, and when we had settled down we were given a couple of days off so that we could have a much-needed rest. It was heaven to sleep in a proper bed for a change, even if they were only double bunks. Mind you, as an NCO in charge of a dormitory I had my own little room and a single bed. I even had a young German soldier who did all my cleaning for me, and I must say he looked after me very well.

When we went into the mess hall for the first time, I noticed through the window that there were a lot of little kids hanging about. When I asked young Hans about this he told that there were gangs of kids roaming round the town, mostly orphans. These children had had to fend for themselves, and they were getting by on scraps of food that they could scrounge. Of course, we had been banned from fraternising with German civilians, but being a dad myself, I couldn't resist filling a bag with food and giving it to them. I did this several times, and got ticked off once or twice, but I suspect that many of our blokes were doing it, even some of the officers. The problem was that once word got round, there were literally hundreds of kids turning up every day, so finally we had to stop it. Thankfully it wasn't long before these poor little perishers were rounded up and taken into care.

The next thing we had to do was to hand our SPs over. I felt quite sad to see them go. We repainted them and they were handed in at Hanover, to be put into storage. The High Command organised a grand handing-over ceremony on 8 June, and we paraded our SPs through the town. General Dempsey and the American General Omar Bradley took the salute. So there we were, pedestrians once more!

By this time the NAAFI had caught up with us, and they established a club for British servicemen in the barracks. We thought this was great, we now had a place where we could relax in the evenings. Our poor old worn-out uniforms and battledress were taken away, and we were issued with new ones, and all new underwear! The nicest thing of all was having proper showers with real hot water.

Inevitably, it wasn't long before the old Bullshit descended on us once more. I hadn't polished my brasses for ages, but of course, it would now be a daily chore. We had daily inspections and parades, and were expected to salute everything that moved, and to paint everything that didn't! Loads of the blokes went out with German girls, even though it was strictly forbidden. It made me sad to see some of my married mates doing it. It was tragic really, some of these girls were practically destitute, and they would give their sexual favours for a couple of cigarettes. Cigarettes were the new currency, replacing the worthless Reichsmark.

One day a party of Russian soldiers turned up to visit us for a few days. They were Marines, and we were told that they were the elite of the Russian

RSM Hector Bennett with General Sir Miles Dempsey at a parade in Hanover, 1945. Courtesy of the Essex Yeomanry.

forces. They were certainly very smartly dressed, and appeared well-disciplined, but after a while we found out that they were all a bunch of wallies! Hardly any of them could read or write, and we discovered that those who could were automatically made NCOs. We took them to our mess hall, and from the way they ate their food you would think they had never seen a knife and fork.

Within a couple of days of their arrival our NAAFI had run short of everything, especially toothpaste. I heard a rumour that they thought toothpaste was some kind of sandwich spread, and that they were putting it on bread and eating it! All the chocolate, the sweets, biscuits, and chewing gum went on the first night they were there, they were buying everything in sight! Apparently they had never seen these goodies before, but they were certainly making up for it. We found out that the Russian Army had no postal service, and no Catering Corps. They just relied on the local people wherever they were stationed to feed them. No wonder they took such a shine to the NAAFI. I don't know how they ever beat the Germans, it must have been simply that they were a tough bunch of blokes. It also became clear that they were completely ruthless in battle, and I was glad that they were on our side.

One day we were assembled in the mess hall, and were told exactly what our duties were going to be. We would be spending our time doing guard duties. There were two main areas of responsibility, guarding the top brass on the *Milwaukee*, and carrying out guard duty at a prisoner of war camp. The latter would require us to fetch German prisoners from the camp and take them to the Intelligence Corps HQ at the main gate for interrogation. In both locations we would be doing twenty-four hours on and twenty-four hours off.

You won't need me to tell you which of those duties I preferred! The guard duty on the *Milwaukee* was mainly ceremonial, and on one occasion when I was Guard Commander, we had a visit from the top Allied Brass. The Guard was turned out for them to inspect, and boy, was I nervous. The VIPs included Montgomery, Bradley, Dempsey, and the infamous General George W. Patton!

General Patton was much shorter than I had imagined, and he was the only one still wearing a steel helmet. Round his waist were his trademark crossed ammunition belts, with holsters carrying his two ivory handled six-shooters. He was very arrogant in appearance, and strutted about as if he was the senior officer on parade. Despite that, he was the only one who seemed really interested in the inspection, and he congratulated me on a good turn-out.

Our other stint of guard duty, the one at the prisoner of war camp, wasn't anywhere near as easy. The prisoners were mainly German officers, and they had to be handled very carefully. Our job was to escort them to the offices occupied by the Intelligence people, but before they were interrogated they were required to take a cold shower, and I mean a cold shower! Most of them took it in their stride, but a few of them were cowards, and kicked up a lot of fuss. One bloke in particular was a little squirt who had been a high-ranking officer at Belsen, so you can guess that we didn't like him all that much. We got him to the shower room, but he didn't want to go under. I don't know what he thought we were going to do to him. We made him strip off, but he refused to take off his long-johns. We had to force him under the shower, and he knelt down and begged for mercy, but we had no sympathy for him. Perhaps he thought that he was going to meet the same fate as some of his victims!

On another occasion we had to go and pick up a Nazi by the name of Schultz. He had been a Gauleiter, which meant that he had been a kind of military Mayor. He had been put in charge of a town in occupied Holland. We went to look for him, taking a German interpreter. This man would act as our spokesman, and would point out who we were looking for.

We approached a group of Germans who were doing some weight training, and our interpreter pointed out a man who was lifting a heavy barbell as if it was a feather. He was huge, well over six feet tall, and we thought that we might have some trouble getting him to co-operate. Not a bit of it, he came with us quite willingly, not a word of protest. When we got him to the shower room he quickly undressed and got under the shower. As he was washing himself, he sang in a lovely baritone voice, and while he was getting dressed he asked me in perfect English if he could borrow my comb. What a contrast!

While the prisoners were undressed, one of our jobs was to look under their arms. If they were SS they would have the SS insignia (two lightning flashes) tattooed in their arm-pits, along with their blood group.

I sometimes wondered if any of our blokes could be as cruel as the Nazis had been, and while I was there, I soon discovered that yes, they could! Unfortunately some of our chaps were thugs. After all that I had seen, I certainly had no love for the Germans, but I drew the line at cruelty. I'm afraid to say that I did witness some really barbaric behaviour. We were armed with a revolver each, and a long cane with a metal knob on the end. I remember seeing one of our sergeants whacking a prisoner on the ankle bones and knees as he marched him from the shower room, and I thought to myself, 'You cruel bastard!' I was never privileged to see inside the interrogation rooms, which was probably for the best, because I don't suppose I would have liked what I saw. I did tell one of our officers about my concerns, but he just shrugged his shoulders and told me to forget it.

29

Home and Away

I had now been awarded a medal, so I wrote home and told my Mum about it. Dear old Mum, she was so excited, she wrote back and told me that she was going to write to the Press about it. Actually, it was the Territorial Army Long Service Medal, not terribly grand, but she went on as if I had won the Victoria Cross or something. I daresay that it was possible that I had given her the wrong idea, young men do sometimes brag to their mothers! I thought, 'Flippin' heck, I'm going to look a right prat if they interview me.' Anyway, she didn't tell them after all, so I was let off the hook.

Frankly, life had become a bit routine, so I was quite glad when I found out that I was to go on leave again. It was a bit of a nightmare journey, most uncomfortable. First of all I went to Cuxhaven, and went on board one of those ships that the Americans had lent us. It was called a Liberty Boat, but I had a completely different name for it, not particularly complimentary. What a rust-bucket! It was more like a tramp-steamer, dirt and rust all over the place, I had very real doubts about its capability of making the crossing to Hull. The journey was scheduled to take thirty hours, so we had sleeping quarters down in the hold. They were just little bunks, in tiers of five. Unluckily I was in a bunk that was right in the middle of a tier, and when I went to bed that night, the bum of the bloke in the bunk above was right in my face!

It was a horrible journey, the ship pitched and tossed all the way. We were very close to Hull, just a few miles away, when we suddenly ran into a thick fog. We had to stop and drop anchor because it was too risky to continue. It was several hours before the fog cleared, allowing us to enter the harbour. I fretted and fumed while we were waiting. I felt quite indignant, here I was, stuck in a dirty old Liberty Boat in the North Sea, when I could have been at home enjoying myself.

It was worth all the trouble though, to get home and see the family once more. It was great to be away from all the Bull, and being able to relax with Lily and the boys took my mind off that ghastly prisoner of war camp.

When I returned to Germany I was relieved to find that another Regiment had taken over our prisoner of war duties. Our new job was nowhere near as difficult, we had to mount a guard on the barracks, and several other important buildings in the town. The job wasn't particularly demanding, so we found ourselves with a lot of leisure time on our hands.

On one of our days off we decided to go down to the beach to have a swim. When we got there we found a rowing boat, so Albert Cardwell, Bert Sherriff, Sam Legge and myself rowed it out to sea. We went out for at least a mile, and we were having great fun. It was a very warm day, and the water looked extremely inviting, so Albert and I decided that we would have a swim. We slipped over the side, and started frolicking about, and we were having such a high old time that we didn't notice what the other two were up to. After a while we thought that enough was enough, and we turned around to swim back to the boat. We were less than amused to see that the other two had started to row back to the beach, leaving us high and dry, or should I say low and wet! They were much too far away for us to catch up, and they ignored our shouts for them to come back. They thought it was hilarious, and they were laughing their socks off, and no amount of swearing, cajoling, or threats would persuade them to wait for us. We were absolutely livid, but there was nothing for it but to swim the mile or so back to the beach.

It took us ages, and we were completely knackered by the time we got there. It was a bloody dangerous thing for Sam and Bert to do, I would have clumped one or both of them had they still been there, but they had had the sense to leg it back to camp. Mind you they didn't get away with it. It doesn't pay to take liberties with the Corporal, as they soon found out. Over the course of the next few weeks I made sure that they got all the dirty, rotten jobs. Oh yes, I got my own back all right!

Many of our officers were from the aristocracy, and some were gentlemen farmers, so riding was second nature to them. Some of them took over a big old house just outside Kiel and formed a country club. Then they had their own horses shipped out from England and stabled them there. It fell to the likes of me to drive over to a big farm near Lubeck to pick up so many bales of hay for the nags.

Now, I knew that the Middlesex Regiment was stationed at Lubeck, so I decided to take the opportunity to visit my brother-in-law and good friend Ned. We had been in the same theatre of war throughout, but had never managed to meet up. So, when it came to my turn to go and fetch the hay, I determined to make a slight detour. I set out to the farm in a fifteen hundredweight truck, and picked up six bales. Then I drove into Lubeck, and drove around until I found the Middlesex Regiment. I found them with no trouble at all, and the Guard Commander directed me to where Ned was billeted. I even found his bed, with a picture of my sister Joyce beside it, but his mates told me that he was home on leave!

Shortly after that I received a letter telling me that Lily was ill. I applied to my CO for some compassionate leave, and he was very kind to me. Not only did he grant me the leave, he also arranged for me to fly home so that I could get to Lily quickly. So off I went with another bloke whose name I can't remember, and reported to the RAF at Lubeck Airport.

God knows how many forms we had to fill in, then they offered us a lift in a freight plane which was going as far as Brussels. The plane was a Dakota, and had a crew of two. The pilot frightened the life out of us by pointing out that the plane was already overloaded, but he said that he would risk it if we would. There were no seats on the plane, and no safety belts, so we just sat down on some boxes and hung on for dear life. I didn't think that the blinking thing was going to get off of the ground, but after a very long take-off run, up we went, skimming the tops of the trees at the end of the runway. The weather was atrocious, and the flight was a bit of a nightmare. Still, we arrived safely at Brussels, and reported to the Airport Transit Office. They gave us tickets for a flight to Biggin Hill in Surrey. Again the plane was a Dakota, and we were grateful to hear that this one was a passenger plane. This time we would have the luxury of seats!

The smiles were soon wiped off our faces when we got on board, because the seats were not arranged in rows, they were placed around the sides of the fuselage facing inwards. It was extremely uncomfortable! Again the weather was terrible, and just after we took off we ran into a terrific storm. The plane pitched and tossed all over the place and we all thought that we were going to crash. There were some WAAFS on board, and they were all screaming their heads off. One of them was clinging on to me, which I daresay would have been quite pleasant under different circumstances!

However, we landed safely at Biggin Hill, and were taken to Victoria by coach. From there it was the familiar bus and train journey via Liverpool Street to dear old Brimsdown, and once more I was home where I belonged.

Poor Lily really was quite ill, she had suffered a nervous breakdown. No one was quite sure how it had come about, but I daresay that bombings, Doodle-bugs, V2 rockets, and the effort of bringing up our three boys without the benefit of having a loving husband by her side were something to do with it. All I can say is, thank God for families. Both of our Mums were so supportive during the war, and Lily's sisters had done a great job of looking after her and keeping an eye on the kids. It also helped that our two families were so close that you would think we were one. It has been one of the great joys of my life that this closeness has continued ever since. Those were dark days, which continued to some extent immediately after the war, and it was comforting to know that if help was needed, it was always just around the corner.

I believe that the role of wives and mothers was grossly underestimated during the war; they did a magnificent job, and there should have been a medal created especially for them. So, I spent these few precious days supporting and comforting my good wife, and also worked on gaining the confidence of three little boys who hadn't seen a great deal of their Daddy!

30

More Guard Duty

We subsequently went back to Kiel, but it wasn't more than a couple of weeks before we found ourselves back on the move once again. Our next task concerned displaced persons, or, as they became known to us, DPs. The Germans had set up hundreds of concentration camps and slave labour camps all over Europe. When the war was over the inmates of these camps had been set free, and the Allies were responsible for returning these DPs back to their own countries.

It was a major operation, the Allies set up transit camps, and the DPs were moved to them before being finally sent home. They had to be examined for illness and injury, and given medical treatment if they needed it, and they also had to be deloused, and clothed and fed. It was a huge task, in fact it took several months. We were instructed to take over guard duty at one of these transit camps just outside of Hanover. This was by no means a piece of cake, because of all the considerable violence that was going on. The majority of the DPs at this camp were either Polish or Russian, and the two races just didn't get on.

There was a violent incident just a couple of days after we had taken over, and as I was on duty at the time, I wound up right in the thick of it. The DPs were lining up for their dinner, and as the food was good and fairly plentiful, our Sergeant Cook didn't mind when some of the men came back for second helpings. However, he put his foot down when several of them came back for third helpings, and he told them off. They responded by setting about him, and they began to give him a right old drubbing. This sparked off the others, and it wasn't long before we had a full-blown riot on our hands. The Guard was called out, so along with all the other blokes on guard duty, I had to wade in to try and quieten them down. Several of the ringleaders were carted off to the Guardhouse, but I don't know what happened to them.

On another occasion we were turned out to put out a fire in one of the huts. Winter in Northern Germany can be pretty cold, but coal was scarce, and had to be rationed. The DPs in this particular hut were not satisfied with their ration, and when they had used it all up they had started chopping up their beds, chairs, tables, and anything else that was made of wood. In no time at all, the hut was on fire. We had to evacuate the DPs while we put the fire out, and while we were busy doing that they raided another hut, turned the occupants out of their beds, piled all the beds up out in the middle of the camp and made a huge bonfire!

They certainly were a handful, those DPs, and we had a hell of a job keeping them under control. We were overjoyed when a lot of them were transferred to another camp! Our living quarters were very comfortable, we had been billeted in a big block of flats just outside the camp. All of the flats had two bedrooms, and some even had bathrooms with showers. We felt very much at home there, and we didn't want to leave, but inevitably we found ourselves on the move again, it was just as well that we were used to it!

The Regiment was ordered to go to Hamburg, but it was several days before I actually got there, because there was a special job to be done. A dozen or so of us were assigned to escort and supervise a trainload of Polish DPs who were going to Stettin, which was in their homeland. I can still remember what an incredibly uncomfortable journey that was. The train was very old, no corridors, no toilets, and the seats were just wooden slats. We took some blankets to sit on, but it didn't help much. The weather was freezing, and there was no heating on the train, so for most of the journey we just sat and shivered. The ground was covered in snow, and when we started off the wheels of the engine were spinning as they tried to get a grip on the rails.

As I mentioned, there were no toilets, and as the journey lasted a whole day, the train had to stop every so often so that the passengers could all relieve themselves. The men all got out one side, and the women got out on the opposite side, and I can still remember looking out of the window with amusement at all the steaming little holes in the snow as the train got underway.

Stettin is right on the Russian/Polish border, and there was a political wrangle going on at the time as to which country the town belonged to. We were billeted for just one night in a big house right on the outskirts, and we were ordered not to go out. The reason for this soon became apparent, because later on that night we could hear the sounds of conflict. As we lay in our beds listening to the sounds of rifle and machine gun fire, I thought, 'Blimey, the war is supposed to be over!'

The next day we made our way to our new barracks in Hamburg, and that journey was no less horrid than the last. It was a real eye-opener as the train reached the outskirts of Hamburg. I was amazed and horrified to see the extent of the bomb damage inflicted by the Allies. It was simply mile upon mile of piles of bricks and masonry rubble. Despite all that had happened, I couldn't help but admire the spirit of the German people as they set about clearing it all up. Men and women were toiling away, side by side, trying to get their city back on its feet. Sights like that did tend to remind me that we all suffer in war!

Our job in Hamburg was pretty cushy, all I had to do was to supervise a squad of blokes ferrying supplies to the NAAFI. Quite frankly, I was bored, so it came as a relief when I was sent on a course. It was something I had always wanted to do, a course on Physical Training. If I passed the practical and written exams I would qualify as a Regimental Instructor, with the possibility of promotion!

31

Physical Jerks!

And so I found myself at the Army Physical Training Centre at Bad Oynhausen. I was one of a hundred other hopefuls, all keen to last the course. We were to be put through an intense, gruelling course of physical training for a week, and those who survived would go on to complete the course proper, which lasted for a further six weeks. I was a bit apprehensive because it seemed very daunting, but I was determined to give it my best shot.

We were issued with track suits as soon as we arrived and we wore them all throughout the course. The food was excellent, and we were fed plenty of red meat, which I loved! We were all given a ration and a half. The first morning we got up at six, put on our track suits and running shoes, and went off on a four and a half mile run. Then it was back to the barracks for a shower and breakfast, and then on parade for nine o'clock. Once parade was over there followed two hours of physical exercises, then lunch, and in the afternoon it was into the gym for training on the vaulting horse, the parallel bars, the wall bars, and floor exercises. The work was hard, but I enjoyed every minute of it.

By the end of that first week I was feeling completely knackered, but curiously, I was beginning at the same time to feel very fit. On the Friday we were all submitted to rigorous passing out tests, designed to see if you were fit enough to carry on for another six weeks. One of the tests was to climb a twelve-foot rope without using your legs, just pulling yourself up by arm power alone. Another test was to carry a man your own weight up a twelve-foot rope ladder and down again. You had to be able to run a hundred yards in under eleven seconds, and a mile in under five minutes. These are the tests that I can remember, but there were plenty of others, all just as demanding!

At the end of that day I was almost too exhausted to move, and I was convinced that the next day I would be on the train going back to Hamburg. The next morning we all rushed over to the notice board to see how we had fared, and we found out that less than fifty percent had passed. To my absolute delight, I saw that I was one of the lucky ones. You would have thought that I would have been relieved, but the first thought that entered my mind was 'Is it really worth all this effort?' It had just dawned on me that now there would be six more weeks of the same! But those six weeks were not anywhere near as bad as the first week, in fact it was very interesting. We still went for our cross-country run early every morning, and we still did our physical exercises, but in the afternoons we covered every other aspect of sport.

We were learning to be Instructors; rather than actually playing, we were taught all the rules and regulations of football, boxing, hockey, competitive swimming, fencing, judo, gymnastics, and athletics. In addition to this we were instructed how to organise events and matches, and were taught how to be referees and umpires.

As Regimental Instructors we would have to put blokes through the dreaded assault courses, so of course, we had to be able to do it ourselves. The course that they had at Bad Oynhausen was a devil, one of the most difficult that I had ever come across, but it did the job, if you could master that one, you were ready for anything!

I also took up serious cross-country running in my spare time, and I often took part in competitions. I enjoyed it, and I don't think that I was bad at it, but I wasn't quite good enough to win any prizes. By this time I was feeling more fit than I have ever been, before or since. I felt as strong as an ox, and I also found that it made me feel aggressive. A lot of the lads felt the same effect, and a lot of them would pick fights with each other and with the locals down at the bars in the town. Thankfully, I managed to stay out of trouble.

Now, you've got to remember that I was still a young man, very fit, and like many young men, particularly those who keep company with other fit and competitive young men, I occasionally let my mouth get me into trouble. The odd slight exaggeration was inevitable when you were trying to impress your peers! However, I paid very dearly for this next indiscretion, as you will see.

We had a boxing instructor by the name of Len Shackleton, perhaps some people will recognise the name, because at one time or another he was middleweight champion of Great Britain. Len had arranged a boxing tournament between us and the Military Police, and to my horror, I found that my name was on the list of competitors representing the Training Centre. You see, some weeks before I had boasted to Len that I was an experienced boxer, never dreaming that I would be called on to prove it! I should have gone to Len and confessed, but I didn't, and so, with much trepidation on my part, came the night of the tournament.

I was to fight a Redcap sergeant, and Len told me that this man was very slow, and that he couldn't take any punishment downstairs. This had cheered me up a bit, because I knew that I had a reasonably hard punch. We both weighed in at eleven stones and ten pounds, and I saw at once that he was much older than me. He also had a bit of a belly, whereas my stomach was flat and hard, and this helped to boost my confidence even more. When the bell sounded for the first round, I went straight for his midriff and gave his belly a real pounding. I expected some reaction, but all he did was to grin at me as he belted me around the ear-hole!

Goodness knows how I got through to the last round, but somehow I did. Suddenly, an opportunity presented itself, and I thought to myself, 'Right, I'm going to finish him off!' I slipped his left lead, and hit him in the solar plexus with the hardest punch I have ever thrown, but to my utter disbelief, it didn't even slow him down. The last thing I remembered was that horrible grin on his face, and the next thing I knew I was coming to in the dressing room. My opponent came over and shook hands with me, saying that I had given him a good fight. I found out later that he was the cruiserweight champion of the British Army! Well, that taught me to keep my mouth shut, and I've never boxed since!

So, the six weeks finally came to an end, and the course terminated with practical tests, and written and oral exams. I passed with honours, and so became a qualified Physical Training Instructor. When I went back to my Regiment they appointed me as their Regimental Physical Training Instructor, and I thought that I might get my third stripe at last. Alas I was to be disappointed, that old misdemeanour kept on coming back to haunt me. It was a bit demoralising to think that I was probably the longest-serving corporal in the British Army. Disappointment aside, I did get a rise in pay, and I was able to wear my Instructor's crossed sabres insignia with pride.

32

The Final Chapter

After eighteen months in Germany I finally became eligible for my demob. I was given the option of signing on again, and although I was enjoying Army life, I felt that I had had enough. I was still a bit disappointed at not getting my third stripe, and besides which, I wanted more than anything to get back to my wife and family.

We were dealt with in groups, and along with all the other eager beavers I was scanning the notice boards every day looking for my group number. After many frustrating delays, the great day finally arrived, and I was given my discharge papers. Among them was a character reference, and I must say that it was very good one, written by my old mate, now Major Warburton. I also drew all my accumulated pay, and a gratuity of sixty pounds. Cor, what a fortune!

I went off to England with mixed feelings, delighted to think that at last I could be with my family permanently, and would be seeing my dear Mum and Dad, my brothers and sisters, and all my friends. At the same time I knew that I would miss all my mates dreadfully. We were more than mates, we were comrades, with all that that word means. We had been through hell together, knowing that we could rely on each other one hundred percent. I have never known the same degree of comradeship since, and I still get a bit misty-eyed when I think of some of those blokes.

I made my way to the Demobilisation Centre at Woking, and there I exchanged my uniform for a navy-blue worsted suit, and a trilby hat. And so I went home via that old familiar route. I got off the train at Brimsdown Station and walked the half a mile or so to Redlands Road. I must have looked quite incongruous striding down Brimsdown Avenue in my posh suit and hat, toting a damn great military kit bag on my shoulder. I remember walking around the corner from Leys Road East into Redlands Road, and seeing a little boy playing on the pavement outside No. 76. I can't remember whether it was Steve or Billy, Michael would have been too little to play outside. Anyway, whichever one it was, he had been told by his Mum that Daddy was coming home, and, bless his little heart, he was waiting to greet me.

So, in I went, with this little tyke hanging round my leg, and I had a wonderful reunion with my family. I blew my gratuity on a holiday at Butlins in Clacton for all of us, just down the road from where I now live! It didn't take me long to get a job, and guess what? I didn't stay out of uniform for long. I rejoined the Territorial Army, based at Tottenham this time, the

Ron's discharge certificate. Courtesy of Mrs L. Davies.

109th Heavy Artillery Regiment. You'd have thought I'd had enough, wouldn't you? Anyway, that elusive third stripe finally came my way, and I became a Gunnery Instructor.

Sad to say, I did lose touch with the Regiment, there were a few letters from some of my mates, and I went to the wedding of one of them. But we were now spread out all over the country, and as the war became just a memory, we gradually lost contact. I did get letters from my surrogate mother Greta Plönes

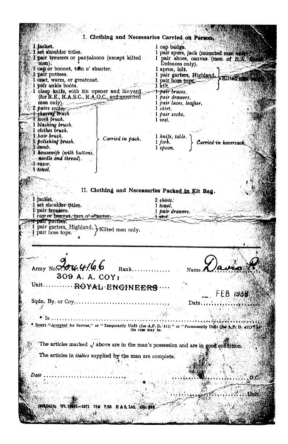

A clothing issue list (embodiment card) RE 309 1938. Courtesy of Mrs L. Davies

in Holland, she wrote to me many times, and we exchanged photographs of our children. Alas, even that finally petered out.

On the positive side, thanks to my sister Betty who lives near Harlow I did re-establish contact with the Essex Yeomanry in recent years, and have been going to reunion dinners with some of my old comrades for some years now. I even discovered that one of my mates, Harry Baker, lives literally a stone's throw away from my son Bill in Frinton! It gave me considerable pride to introduce my family to those old comrades of mine, and they were tickled to meet Lily, my sons, and one of my grandsons! It was quite amusing to be called Popeye again!

As I may already have mentioned, I contacted Betsje and Chrisje Plönes through the Regiment, and Lily and I went with Bill and his wife Sylvie to Holland, and spent some time as their guests. It was wonderful to see those two middle-aged ladies, and to talk about the times we spent together. They still remembered 'Der Grosse Caporal!'

But the thing that pleased me most was going over to Normandy nearly fifty years after that fateful day in June 1944. It was the year before the official fiftieth

Betsie and her husband Franz with Ron, Lily, Sylvie and Bill, 1999. By Bill Davies.

Ron with General
Richardon at the reunion in
2000. By Bill Davies.

Chris with Bill and Sylvie, 1999. By Bill Davies.

anniversary D-Day celebrations. Sylvie and Bill thought it might be a good idea to go over before the area became overcrowded with tourists.

We went to Arromanches, and there were the old Mulberry harbours, still in place! We went on to Le Hamel, and although it had changed out of all recognition, I still managed to find the exact spot where we had come ashore all those years ago. Nearby I found an old gun emplacement, and on it was a plaque dedicated to the men of the Essex Yeomanry who had given their lives on that day. It was a sad, but proud moment for me. I will also readily confess that I shed more than a few tears when I walked around the military cemetery in Bayeux. Row upon row of little white crosses, and I worked out that the average age of our dear fallen comrades was around twenty-one. Those men were heroes, and I find it a little sad that the world sometimes forgets them. I never will.

THE END

Rom at Le Hamel beach, 1993. By Bill Davies.

The Essex Yeomanry memorial at Le Hamel, 1993. By Bill Davies.

Reunion at Harlow, 2000. Courtesy of General Richardson.

LETTERS

Date: Summer 1942

Address: A Troop
413 Battery
Essex Yeomanry
Ilfracombe
Devon

My own sweet, darling Lily,

Well, here we are at the seaside. I don't think a great deal of it because it's done nothing but rain since we've been here. I'm on guard at the present and am I feeling cheesed off, but you will be pleased to know that I'll be home on Weds week. I got the 6 o'clock train alright darling, and the fare came within my pocket. As soon as I got back I came on down here with some of the lads. We came by train, and what a journey it was. All in the darkness, and we had our full kit plus blankets to carry. We've got pretty good billets. It used to be a big hotel.

There are thousands of Yanks here, and do they make whoopee! You should hear them! Oh well dear, I must buzz off for now, because I'm on guard and, I've only got a few minutes before I'm on duty. So I'll say cheerio my sweet and remember, I love you with all my heart. God bless and keep you safe 'til Wednesday week

Your loving Hubby

Ron

x x x x x x x
x x x x x x x
x x x x x x x x x x
x x x x x x x x x x

Date: November 1945

Address: Bdr R.A.Davies 2044166
P.T. School No 3 Sec
BAOR Training Centre
BAOR

My own sweet darling,

here I am, at it again, God knows why I do it but I do and I know I should be ashamed of myself. I could make excuses but I won't. You may not believe it, but I've written more in the last week than I've done all my life. We have to take notes on everything we do here, I'll show 'em to you one day. But I know I should have written darling, and I'm sorry.

But honestly dear, this is a gruelling course, and although I'm determined to finish it, I'm fed up with it. I feel fit mind you, and it has obviously done me some good. They want me to go to Aldershot for a course and become a Sergeant-Instructor in the APTC but I've turned it down because it would mean me signing on for another year, which I won't do. I've had enough of it. I did a silly thing the other day dear. I happened to mention that I've done a little boxing before and they put me straight in for a fight which I fought Friday night. I fought as a middleweight and I was surprised when I weighed in at eleven stone six pounds. Anyway, I won fairly easily and now I have to fight again for the School on Tuesday night. I got a nice little wallet on Friday though, but I don't intend to keep it up, I don't like it much.

We have a lot to do here you know dear. We're on the go from nine 'til five, and we can't smoke during that time, so you can guess, I'm gradually cutting my smoking down. Sometimes we go out to local units and take them on at PT and it's not so easy. One good thing though, a PT Instructor can always find a good job in Civvy Street. I know a bloke for instance who instructs his local Police Force in his spare time for six bob an hour. Another got a job at a school at five quid a week! So, these five weeks aren't really wasted, are they? It's only this place that gets me down. I haven't set foot outside the place since I've been here except when we've been out for runs. That's another good thing dear, I ran five miles yesterday without stopping and I never got out of breath. Also, last week I walked five miles in fifty minutes, which is really good going.

Every sport under the sun is taught here and there are professionals here to teach us. There are Americans here to teach us American games, again, useful. On top of all that we learn ju-jitsu, fencing, boxing, wrestling, and other rough sports. Then there is the PT itself which is tough.

Still darling, you don't want to hear about that, do you? I hope the kids are a bit better. I can't understand it myself, because they seemed alright when I left. Maybe it's the excitement of Christmas coming, I wish I could be there for it darling. Think of the next one though dear, what a time we'll have.

I think that your idea of a Holiday Camp is a good one, I'm all for it, so we'll go. As much as I love the kids I wish that we could go alone, but that would hardly be fair, would it? We could have a real good time together, couldn't we? You'll have to book up early dear,
so that we can have a good chance of getting a place. I want you to have a good time dear, because you haven't had much enjoyment during the last six years. I'll make up then for all the letters I haven't written, and you'll find I do love you, well and truly.

So far my example of being a good husband hasn't been very good. But time will tell, and really darling, I'm a good husband at heart. I'm just thoughtless, that's all. It's being away from you that does it, although I never forget about you, please believe that dear. I have so many sweet memories to look back on, and I could write for hours about them. We had some lovely times in the past and will have many more in the future. I've been telling you for over six years now that I love you, but I'll tell you again because you like me to. I love you darling with all my heart and I'll love you till I die. You've always been my girl and you always will. No other can ever take your place in my heart dear, there is no room.

So you see dear, April simply must come quick because I'm longing for you. I want to kiss you and tell you how much I love you, and how sweet you are. No need for any more blasted letters, and no more worry. I can't see why we shouldn't live a perfectly normal happy life together, and I shall make it my duty to see that we do, we'll have our little tiffs I suppose, but we won't let them develop into anything worse, will we dear. As long as you love me and I love you, nothing can go wrong. We've got to see the kids alright too. I don't want them to make the mistakes I have so it's up to us to see that they don't. They must learn a trade for one thing, which is one thing I should have done. Still, time will tell.

Well dearest, I must sign off for now. So remember I love you and adore you darling, and I'm longing for a chance to prove it. Good night darling, love to the kids, and God bless you all.

Your loving and longing
Ron

x Billy   x x x x x x x x x x x
x Stevie   x x x x x x x x x x x
x Michael   x x x x x x x x x x x

Date: November 1945

Address: Bdr R.A.Davies 2044166
PT School no 3 Section
BAOR Training Centre
BAOR

My own sweet darling,

here we are again dear, all merry and bright. I feel as fit as a fiddle, and I only wish I could be home to show you. Last night I fought and won a prize, and as usual, Joe Soap got into the finals, and then lost. I won my first scrap, but the second bloke was too heavy for me, and although I hit him hard, and got him groggy, I couldn't knock him out and in the finish I tired myself out hitting him and he got the better of me. Still, I enjoyed it, and I got forty fags so it wasn't too bad was it?

They've turned me into a proper acrobat here darling and it's done me the world of good and I'm glad I came in a way. I only hope that when I get back they will let me carry on so that I can keep myself fit. Because it's obvious if I just let myself get lazy I shall have wasted my time here. I've worked damn hard to get myself fit and I don't want to go back to my old standard of fitness.

Well darling, how is everything at home? How are the boys, any better? I'm just longing to get home again dear. I might just scrape another leave in before I'm demobbed. It won't be very long now dear. Xmas is almost here and before we know where we are it will be nineteen forty-six. I feel so impatient at times. God only knows what sort of a Xmas we'll get here. I know you won't have a good one dear. I wish I could be home for it, perhaps we could have enjoyed it more. I know what we'll get. A pint of tinned beer, tinned turkey, and a bit of tinned Xmas pudden! Still, I'm not worried much about what I get, it's just the thought of not having you with me. I really would enjoy myself then. I always do when you're with me. I don't know for the life of me what I shall do for Xmas presents dear. We can't get anything out here, not even Xmas cards, so don't be disappointed dear if you don't get one, will you. I wish I could get the kids something but I don't suppose I'll be able to. Anyway, I will try my best.

Well I must close now dear, so I'll say good night. I love you so very much dear and I long for you with all my heart. God bless you darling angel and keep you safe.

Always your loving
Ron

X Billy   x x x x x x x x
X Stevie   x x x x x x x x
X Michael   x x x x x x x x
(bless 'em!)

Date: 13 December 1945

Address: Bdr R.A.Davies 2044166
A/413/147th Field Regt RA
EY (TA)
BAOR

My own sweet darling,

just a note darling to let you know that I've nearly finished my course and I shall soon be back with the Regiment. As far as I know I've passed ok but anyway I don't much care if I haven't. I'm fed up with life, although I shouldn't be I know. I've got everything a man could wish for, a home, a family, and a wife to love me, and to whom I can tell all my troubles. Once

I get back dear and I don't write then I really do deserve ticking off, so help yourself, won't you.

You'll have to excuse my scribble, I can hardly stand up. We've had a bashing today, and will get an even bigger one tomorrow. Just wait 'til I get back to the Regiment, someone will have to pay for this.

I think that you can expect me home in March now dear, I see they've speeded the demob up. About time too, only it should be a bigger speed-up. I don't suppose that I shall get another leave now.

Well darling, how is everybody at home. Kids alright? What kind of a Xmas will you have; not so good, I'll bet. I don't know what it will be like here, in any case I'm not worried because I shan't enjoy it anyway. I didn't forget the baby's birthday dear, but what could I do? There's nothing I can send him, not even a card. Wait until next year, he'll be almost old enough to appreciate a birthday. We'll be able to make up for all these little things won't we dear. How I wish I could have been a bit more of a better husband but it's too late now. I'll just have to try to make it up later on.

Well dear, I must close now or else drop, so I'll say cheerio for now. I'll always love you darling with all my heart. God bless you dear and take care of yourself.

Yours for ever
Lovingly
Ron
x x x x

Date: 19 December 1945

Address: Same old mob!
Same old bloke!

My own sweet darling,

I've just got back to the Regiment again dear, and am I glad. No more PT for me, I passed the course ok, and nearly passed out myself too! Really though dear, I feel as fit as a fiddle, it has done me the world of good. Well sweet, it's Xmas, and I've got nothing to offer you. I've still got that coffee, and so far I haven't been able to get a watch for you, but I'm still trying.

I sent off five pounds this morning, will that be alright? I wouldn't send postal orders as they might get pinched being Xmas time, so I sent it through the Post Office Enfield Highway. Twenty-five Group will be starting on Jan 4th so it won't be long now, will it dear. I think my group starts on March 10th so that's only about three months isn't it. I don't suppose that I shall get another leave in, but I might. Roll on March!

Do you think we'll be able to manage that trip to the holiday camp darling, or will it be too early? I hope we can go because I'm looking forward to our first holiday together. We've never had one, and I want to see you enjoying yourself like you deserve to do. Perhaps I can show you that I'm not such a bad husband after all.

How are the kids dear. Are they excited at the thought of Xmas? I wish I could see their little faces on Xmas morning. I feel so rotten not being able to send them anything. Still, next year it will be different. So far we don't know anything about our Xmas here. We might have a good one, but I doubt it very much, although the officers have got quite a do on so I'm told.

Remember I told you I was having a drawing done of you? Well I got it today. It's not too bad, and I'll send it on to you. It doesn't make you as good-looking as you really are though, but it's a good drawing. Will you do me a favour dear. I'm a qualified PT Instructor now and I get an extra threepence a day for it, so I'm entitled to wear the crossed swords, so will you see if you can get me a couple of pairs. That shop in Edmonton have got some I know. It doesn't matter if they're brass ones or cloth ones. Our CO is very touchy on these things and he tells you off if you don't wear your badges of office.

Well darling, I must close now. Have a good Xmas won't you, and try to enjoy yourself. I love you so very much darling and I'm longing for March to come so that I can hold you in my arms, knowing that I need never let you go. A very Merry Xmas and a Happy New Year to Mum and the girls and all my love and wishes and longing for you dearest. God bless you darling, and take care of yourself.

Yours ever loving and
longing
Ron

X X X
Xmas kisses for the kiddies
bless their little hearts – I love them too

Date: late December 1945

Address: Not given

My own sweet darling,

well dear, that's that, Xmas is over, and thank the Lord it is. I got gloriously drunk and now I must suffer. I fell down the stairs and done something to my knee. We don't know whether it's broken or not, but I can just about walk so I don't think it is, but blimey it's sore. What a way to finish Xmas. You'll be pleased to know that I'll be home on the 18th January. Not for good, I've wangled another leave. That is if my knee gets better in time. It won't be so very long now before I'm out for good so another leave will shorten it a bit won't it darling.

How did the kids get on at Xmas? I'd love to have been there to see their faces. Did you enjoy yourself dear? I did, up 'til I remember. We had a good dinner and tea, and then we really started. I had Boxing Day in bed though, I felt terrible after I cracked my knee. I'm still hobbling about though. I was playing football too today. Curses, why do things happen to me always, I wish I had someone I know to take care of me. That's what I need I think.

By the way dear, don't forget my crossed swords will you. I want them for a special reason. Well dear, I was going to send some postal orders to you, but I'd better keep it until I come home. It'll be safer. I've sent you these few odds and ends you might like. There is also your picture, I had it done. It's not a lot like you dear, but it's not bad. You're really much lovelier.

Well, I must close now dear, but remember the 18th January, are you for it? So good night dear and God bless. I love you with all my heart.

Yours for ever
Still loving and longing
Ron

x x x x x x x x x x x x x x
x x x x x x x x x x x x x x
x x x x x x x x x x x x x x

Date: 31 December 1945

Address: Same old bloke
Same old place

My own sweet darling,

just a note dear in answer to your letter that I got today. I'll be home on Jan 18th so you'll have to stick up with me for another twelve days. I'm bringing some hooch home too, so we'll get drunk shall we? My leg is much better now and I can walk without limping, so you can't call me Hopalong now, can you? I had a letter from Dad today and he's quite serious about our little idea. Well, to be quite frank dear, I'm not going back to the Co-op, so I think I should try Dad's idea out for a while. It should work out ok, and I hope it will pay. I want you to have more money if I can. I don't want you to have to live as you have been, and it's my duty to see that you don't. What do you think darling, should I go in with Dad? I'll take your decision as final dear. What do you say?

Got over Xmas yet? I have. There's a little celebration tonight, but I'll save my drink. Think of me at 12 o'clock dear, I'll be thinking of you and I'll be wishing you a very happy New Year. I'll be hoping your husband will be home with you for good very soon.

I'm glad you got the money ok dear. It didn't get home in time though, did it? It's been pretty miserable here lately. Bags of rain and snow, and baby, is it cold! Brrrr! If you have a pee it freezes as it comes out! I've never been so cold in all my life. I'll be warm when I get home though, in more ways than one.

Well darling, I'll have to close now so I'll say goodnight for now. I love you very much darling and I'm longing for you. God bless you darling, and a Happy New Year.

Yours forever
Loving and longing
Ron

X For Billy   x x x x x x x x x x x x x x x x
X For Stevie   x x x x x x x x x x x x x x x x
X For Michael   x x x x x x x x x x x x x x x x
(Bless 'em!)

Date: 3 January 1946

Address: "The Looney Lover"
"Looney Bin"
"Colney Hatch II"

My very own sweet darling angel,

I love you, I love you, and still I love you. I know I'm crazy but I just can't help it, I'm crazy for you baby. What a gal! You know darling every time I look at this photo in front of me you seem to grow more and more lovely, and I'm not kidding.

Your mother did a wonderful thing when she brought you into this world and I want to thank her from the bottom of my heart, so do you know what I've done? I've sent your Mum some flowers. Not much of a gift, but flowers are beautiful, and so is my wife. I asked for roses, but it doesn't matter what they are, I know that sweet old lady will appreciate them. Cost me something, but what does money matter where love is concerned. If you get this letter first darling you won't tell her, will you? Would you like some dear? I can get them sent tomorrow if you like. I think I will anyway.

It's a new scheme darling, we order the flowers, pay for them, and they are delivered to whoever you wish, anywhere in the British Empire, nice isn't it? I wanted to send your Mum some orchids but they were £2 each so I asked for roses. I like roses, don't you? You must think I've gone all romantic all of a sudden but I just happened to think of your dear old Mum lying there and I thought I'd like to do something for her, so as I can't get any gifts out here, I thought of flowers. I know Mum likes them and I know she'll understand the message that they convey. I want you to know darling that I've always had a little spot in my heart specially for her, and I love her for just being your mother and not only that because she is so sweet and brave. I mean that dear with all my heart, I really do.

Another reason why I'm so loving tonight is because I'm thinking of my leave, which won't be very long now. It looks like everyone will be home soon except for little me, but never mind honey, it won't be long now. What a day! Just to get out of this khaki and into some real clobber.

Well my sweet one, I must sign off now just for a while. I'll write again soon, I'm in the mood. Don't say it, I know it doesn't seem possible, but all the same darling I feel happier tonight than I've been for a long time, and I do love you so much sweet, honest I do. Goodnight my darling, and God bless you, and the babes. I love them too bless 'em.

Yours for always
and
loving you for ever
Ron

x x x x x x x x x x x
x x x x x x x x x x x
x x x x x x x x x x x

PS: I may have a little surprise for you soon dear and DON'T FORGET MY X SWORDS THEY'RE 30d A DAY EXTRA and I do love you dear.

Date: c.9 January 1946

Address: Same Place
Same Time
Same Bloke

My own sweet darling,

just got your letters sweet, and thanks for the swords, I'll forgive you this time, but don't let it happen too often otherwise I shall have to kiss you to death. Well darling, it won't be long now, will it? I leave here on Wednesday so I'll be home about dinner-time on Saturday. Providing the weather holds out.

So get some grub in dear, won't you. If you think you'd like something strong to drink then just you wait until you taste this stuff I've got. I don't think I'll let you drink it neat. It'll only burn your insides out, but it's a lovely feeling. But if I get drunk, you'll be twisting _me_ around _your_ finger. Then I shall be doing things a gentleman wouldn't, but who the hell wants to be a gentleman anyway? We'll have to be careful though, because if we do get drunk I can see us winding up with a baby daughter yet.

Now, about the flowers darling. I went up to send them and they told me that they sometimes take two or three weeks to get home so I might be home before they arrive. So I never sent you any, it wasn't worth it. Your Mum's should arrive sometime this week I hope.

Well darling, how's the weather at home, I did hear there was a gale blowing. It's not too bad here, but it's been terribly cold. Life still carries on the same here, and the Jerries are getting a bit out of hand at times, but we manage them ok. They really are hard up you know dear. They will do almost anything for a few fags or a bit of grub. I'm certain that there's not a virgin left in Kiel. The girls hang about all over the place just waiting for a bloke to pick them up. This place is lousy with VD and almost every day someone has to go off to the Hospital with it. It makes me shudder to think about it. If ever I were daft enough to get it I'd never come home again. I wouldn't be able to face you dear. I'd do myself in. But I won't get it, so let's change the subject shall we dear. Let's talk about love, our love.

Can you remember the first time I told you that I loved you? Can you? I was a twerp, wasn't I, and you were a vamp, yes you were, you got round me and coaxed me into saying it. Not that I didn't want to say it, I did, but I couldn't get it out. Can you remember our first kiss darling. We'd just come back from the dance and it was pouring with rain and you looked so lovely standing there with your hair in rats tails all over your face. Who could have resisted the temptation to kiss you. You were so lovely darling, and you still are. What about the night when I forgot to make a date? Whew, you were worried. Then there was the day when you were knocked down by that motor-bike. I was on the verge of tears that day, honest I was. I'd have throttled that bloke if I could have seen him.

Oh, there are hundreds of sweet memories to look back on aren't there dear? I'll bet I could write a book about them. Maybe I will one day. And now after six long years we're still together and very much in love, more so than ever before. Being away has made me realise how very much I do love you darling. I often wonder how it is that I'm here at all. I must have had Lady Luck looking down on me for years. She certainly was looking down on me when I decided that Lily Hussey would be Lily Davies. It was a lucky break for me. I shall always consider that as the greatest honour ever bestowed on me and I shall be forever grateful. Not that I deserve you dear. You've stuck by me through thick and thin and you have been so faithful and loyal to me. I love you for that dear and I want you to know that whatever happens I'll never never lose love and respect for you. I'll love you forever dear and I'll really try to show it this time.

Well, I've said enough for the present dear, so I'll close. Goodnight darling, take care of yourself and roll on Saturday. God bless you Angel, you're a real pal, and I love you so much it aches.

Yours for ever and ever
Lovingly
Ron

X They'll soon   x x x x x x x x x
X be all x x x x x x x x x
X over me   x x x x x x x x x

Date: 12 February 1946

Address: Bdr R.A.Davies 2044166
A Battery
98th Field Regt RA
BAOR

My own sweet darling,

well darling, as you can see, I've been posted at last. We arrived here last night so I can't tell you much about the place. All I know is that it's called Ahrensbock, and it's just a tiny village, just outside Lübeck. There are quite a few of our lads here so at least I have company. Albert never came though. I think he's going to some other Regiment. This is really only a holding place for us actually until our demobs come, so we are still in the EYs and are only attached to this mob. We won't be here for long. For in another four weeks the twenty-sevens start rolling, and if I'm lucky I might get drawn out of the hat first but in my case six weeks will see me in Civvy Street.

I've signed my release book and forms, and I've seen my character, which even if I do say so myself is pretty good. I also had my medical and I was a bit worried about my knee. You see dear some of the boys get deferred so that they can get their injuries better. But our Doctor examined my knee very closely and he said that I had no need to worry about it. He even said that in time I should be able to play Football again. But I've got to watch it and make sure I don't put too much strain on the muscles, otherwise it will never get better. He said massage would do it good.

Well darling I'm afraid I can't send you ten bob this week. We're not settled in yet and I don't know the routine here yet, but as soon as I can find out I'll let you know, and send it on. How's young Billy, any better? I wonder if he's got the Flu like everybody else. I was bad dear. I only got up the day before yesterday, and I still feel shaky, but I shall be bright in a day or two. You know when I had my teeth out, well I've cursed that day. I've got a perishing abscess or something on one of my toothless gums and it isn't half sore.

Well darling, I must close now. Remember dear, only four weeks, and no more of this. What a relief that will be. I love you so much my sweet and it seems so long since I held you close. But it won't be long now, will it. So darling, cheerio for now and God bless. I love you sweet.

Yours forever
Lovingly
Ron

x x x x x x
x x x x x x x
x x x x x x x
x x x x x x
x x x x x

Date: 23 February 1946

Address: Bdr R.A. Davies 2044166
A Battery
98th Field Regiment RA
BAOR

My own sweet darling,

well dear, I've moved again. I've been attached to the Military Government in Oldenburg which is the most northern town on the Baltic coast. Before very long, almost by the time you get this, I shall be off again somewhere else. Since I've been back off leave I've been mucked about more than I have been in six years. The snag is mail. When we get to know where we're going we can't write because we don't know the address, and we can't write before that you see because we don't even know where we're going. So it's all one big muck-up, and as far as I can see this kind of thing will carry on until my time is up, which thank the Lord is very close.

Do you know how many of your letters I've had so far dear? One, and that had three different addresses on it, although I'm hoping for another one very soon, 'cos I daresay you have written more. You see dear, by the time you get this I shall be gone, then your letter will go to my last place Ahrensbök, then they'll come here to Oldenburg, then to the next place, and where that is God only knows, then probably I shall be off again, so darling, as you can see, it's rather difficult, isn't it? I hope you'll understand dear. I don't want you to think that I'm deliberately neglecting you. I've done too much of that in the past and now I'm trying my hardest to make up for it.

I've only got one ambition now dear, and that is to make you content and happy. I want you to have everything you want. We'll make a success of this marriage yet. Well darling, how are things at home? Are the kids any better? They all seemed under the weather when I left. Are you alright yourself dear? I've still got a terrible cold dear, and if you could hear my voice you'd think that I'd swallowed a sheet of sand-paper. I'm just like an old frog.

Well my darling Angel, I must close now, duty calls. Before I do I want you to know that you're the best girl in all the world and I wouldn't part with you for all the tea in China, and darling, I love you with all my heart and soul, and I ain't kidding. Sometimes the longing I get for you hurts so much I could almost cry. So sweetheart, cheerio for now, God bless you, and He knows I love you.

Yours for ever
Loving you always
Your own
Ron

X For the kids   x x x x x x
I love them   x x x x x x
too   x x x x x x

Date: 12 March 1946

Address: Bdr R.A.Davies
2044166
A Battery
98th Field Regt
BAOR

My own sweet darling,

please don't think too badly of me dear, even though it may seem I'm not thinking of you, I am. It seems that fate doesn't want you to have too many letters. I'm browned off as hell, and I'd willingly choke somebody. I don't know whether I'm on my head or my heels at the moment. One day I'm in one place and the next day miles away. At present I'm in a place called Neustadt and once again, by the time you get this, I shall be off again.

It's Münster this time which is a hell of a way from here. Your letters keep on following me around. Yesterday I had three from you, one letter and two packets of fags. Thanks darling, I needed them. Another snag is I can't draw any postal orders of any kind because they take a week to come through, and as fast as I order them they shift me off beforehand.

I want my boots repairing and numerous other little jobs done, but I can never get settled down long enough to get them done. Well dear, it's getting very near demob time. Only five days and it will be the 17th. I don't know my release date yet but I hope to know in a few days time. Oh, I'm praying for an early date. Keep your fingers crossed darling.

Of course we can afford the holiday dear. If we don't go now we might not get another chance for ages, so let's take this opportunity to get a holiday while we can, you need a holiday dear, and God only knows you deserve one. And besides, we've never had a honeymoon, so this is it. Where shall we go dear? I'm afraid I shall have to let you make all the arrangements darling, but you can do that can't you.

We'll have two weeks just pleasing ourselves, and darling, we'll make up for everything. It'll be a change for you dear, no housework, no cooking, and no waiting for letters from your old man, so sweet, it should do you the world of good, and I'm looking forward to seeing you really happy and enjoying yourself.

Well sweet, I must close now, but I will (I know I've said this before) I will write again as soon as possible. I do love you darling, you know that don't you. So good night my darling and God bless you.

Your ever loving
And adoring
Ron
x x x x x x x x x
x x x x x x x x x
x x x x x x x x x
x x x x x x x x x
x x x x x x x x x
X For the nippers,
bless 'em

Date: 24 *March* 1946

Address: Bdr R.A. Davies (Nearly Mister)
A Troop 391 Battery
98th Field Regt RA
BAOR

My own sweet darling,

Won't be long now dear. By the time you get this I'll only have three or four days to go before I leave here. What a relief it will be to get on that boat for the last time. No more coming back, no more goodbyes, and no more letters.

I got you letter today and I'm ever so pleased you didn't take that letter of mine seriously. Honestly darling, I really didn't mean it. I'd felt niggly all day and I had to let off steam at someone. I hope you'll forget it dear, will you? Please darling?

You would laugh if you could see me now dear. I'm in a hell of a condition. I can hardly see to write this. I've been at it again, you know, boxing. I did say I wouldn't do it any more, but I was forced into it. As usual I came off second best, as a result, not one black eye, but two! I hope they'll wear off by next Sunday. But I got a lovely fountain pen as second prize, fourteen carat gold it is, and it's a smasher, honest. If you're a good girl I might give it to you for your birthday. Oh, and darling, I must make a confession. I did forget poor Billy's birthday. I'm sorry dear, it just went out of my head. My mind is full of only one thing at the moment, and you can guess what that is. I wouldn't have missed it for worlds. I'll make it up to him when I come home. Tell him, won't you.

I'm glad Ned and Joyce can come with us on our holiday, and I must say that I'm really looking forward to seeing you enjoy yourself for once in a while. Where are we going anyway? You never told me. I hope we'll have enough money darling, although we should manage alright.

Our Group may have to wait for our civvy suits, we shan't know for sure, so I might have to buy myself one to go away with, so I'll have to reserve a little money for that won't I. You know dear, you'll have to watch Ned and I, once we get inside a camp again we may be doing all sorts of odd things.

You know darling, it's odd how you can miss an old pal. I'm lost without old Albert, and according to his letter which I got today, he feels the same. He's got another Group to go yet. He should have been with me, but he's done detention, so he's got to wait. I wish you could have met him dear, you'd have liked him. He wishes to be remembered to you dear, and he sends lots of love to the boys. I've heard from Dick Munsen too, and he gets demobbed on the same day as me. With luck I might meet him. I hope so anyway. He gets marries soon and he says he hopes to see us in the near future.

Well darling, I must close now. I don't suppose you'll get many letters now, so hold on to your hat, I'm a comin' honey! I'm longing to see your face when I walk in that door, a free man. You're wonderful Angel and I love you with all my heart and soul. Goodnight sweetheart, and God bless you.

Yours forever
Lovingly
Ron

x x x x x x x x
x x x x x x x x
x x x x x x x
x x x x x x x

X Bless their
little hearts

Date: 5 January 1945

Mrs Davies,

I introduce me, alls the seconds mother of Ronny your houseband. — He is our best friend. He came two times on holiday to my home and he is here like a son in the house.

   He says all the time to me, you is my second Mummy, my Mummy in Holland. My three children, they like him like their own father, and Ronny he likes them almost so much like his own boys. Mrs Davies, when you may will you send me a foto of your boys please? That makes us happy. The foto of your wedding day is in our living room in all the best places. And the foto of Ronny and Billy too. When Ronny come the first time he show it to me before three minutes, the fotos of you all.

   His wife and his boys is to him all the world. Ronny come with holiday, and he went with the children to play in the street. They come in at five o'clock and it was dark, and we think, now we see him a little time. Snow was laid, and they all like snowmans when they come in. The children find the snow very nice and Ronny too.

   Your houseband, he do know it that I write to you. Do yourself write to him? Good? I find it nice. You too? I hope so. When you can you write me please back?

With the kindest regards

From Ronny's Holland Mummy

Gretha Plönes
My houseband Alfred

And the children, Betsy, Chrisje, and Freddy

(I hope we see you soon)

April 18th- 4-46

My friend Billy

I received your nice letter the 13 April, and what shall everybody glad now your father is home for good. Jes Billy. You was one year old, when there was war. And now you are six or seven years old. You must feel you proud now don't you? Now you can play and walk with your father and mother Steve and Marcel. And no more go away, and no more crying for your mother, when your papa was leaving; if he has to go to Germany. Billy you wrote that your papa will write so you can tell from now, that he has time to write in a little letter. Billy your mother will send Betsy and Chrisje a souvenir from England. I know that every thing cost much money. I don't like that your mother think. Now the Dutch people ask so much as English people. Betsy birthday is 20 April. And she has no strange for in her hair I hope you understand me. This for her hair or her long hair. Now if it isn't too much I will ask you if you can get a band for in her hair. I didn't ask before But for this time I will try I know you smile at and wen if somebody has birthday and then you like some thing to have. Betsy wear her hair in two long strang on her I do she wear also as strange. Now I hope Billy that you

The first page of Greta's original letter, dated 18 April 1946. Courtesy of Mrs L. Davies.

Date: 18 April 1946

My friend Billy,

I received your nice letter the 13th April, and how shall everybody be glad now your father is home for good. Yes Billy, you was one year old when there was war. And now you are six or seven years old. You must feel you proud now. Don't you?

Now you can play and walk with your Father and Mother, Stevie and Marcel, and no more go away, and no more crying for your Mother when your Papa was leaving if he has to go to Germany. Billy you wrote to me that your Papa will write to me. You can tell him now that if he has time he can write in a little letter. Your Mother has promised to send Betsy and Chrisje a souvenir from England. I know that everything cost so much money. I don't like that your Mother think now the Dutch people ask so much on English people.

Betsy birthday is 20th April and she has no band for her hair. I hope you understand me. This is for her to tie back her hair. Now if it is not so much I will ask for if you can get a band for in her hair. I didn't ask before but for this time I will try. I know you understand and when if somebody has a birthday and then you like something to have. Betsy wearing her hair in two long strands on her back. Now I hope Billy that your Mother not feel bad if I ask for that; if I get those bands for Betsy. Chrisje and Freddy they happy too.

My poor Mother died on 30th March. She was heartsick. Yes that is very bad if you lost your Mother too soon. Papa goes again from 10th April on working at the mine. Now Billy, Stevie and Marcel, maybe we will see you when you come to Holland in 1947.

We are all happy now. I hope you don't get mad because I ask you for that. Lily and Ronny, you know I ask for Betsy. She was always Ronny's best friend, and she was always playing with him.

Greetings from your friends in Holland
Alfred and Gretha

If you can get the band before Betsy's birthday will you try please.

Good luck, so long.

Greetings from al and will you write back please.

Heerlen , Nov. 13 th

Dear Ronnie and Lily,

Last week i've got a call from Mientje Willems from the Plataanplein.
She told me that your son Bill was trying to find the family Plones.
You see , he found me.
After this long time , how are you and lily and your sons .
Now i tell you something about us.
Dad (pap) is dead for 12 years, Mam is dead for 8 years and Freddie is dead for 5 years.
Cristel is already 63 years old , not married but enyoing life by traveling around the world a lot.
Now me Betsie ; I'm 65 years old , happely married to Frans also 65 years old.
Whe have two sons , Albert and Fred . Both married to good wives Anita and Sonja
Albert works as a policeman and has two daugthers Esther and Ingrid.
Fred works at the dutch railway (N.S.) at the office and also two daugthers Rachelle and Mirthe.
You see that we have four lovely grandchildren who loves to be with theire grandparents.
Ronnie , with this letter you find a copy of a passage in my poetryalbum that you wrote.
I can remember you so well and it was a great time when you where at our house.
Ronnie , after i heard from the letter your son send , i called someone you also know, do you remember Jan van der Heiden, my neighbour , he wishes you all the best.
Mam and i talked a lot about you , when you came home dirty again and you had to wear the clothes of pappa or that time that mam learned you the word ROTMOF and you didn't know what it mend.
I remember me also when mam was mad at you about the dirty clothes, you sad down in the kitchen under the mirror , you fould your hands behind your head and song , if i remember well Ave Maria . Than here bad mood was over and she always song about Lily Marleen to tease you.
Ronnie i'll hope that we will see and hear from you.
Your also welkom to stay when your in Holland (grose korporaal)
Greetings from all of us and please write us back soon because i would find this great.

Greetings Betsie en Frans Diwisch-Plones

Tel: 003145725927
Delftstraat 16
6415 BN
Heerlen
The Netherlands

A letter from Betsie Diswich-Plönes, dated 13 November 1998. Courtesy of Mrs L. Davies.

THE NORMANDY INVASION, JUNE 1944

D-DAY TO D-DAY + 7

[Taken from the article by Major General T.A. Richardson CB MBE in the *Journal of the Royal Artillery*]

231 Brigade was the right-hand assault brigade of 50th Northumbrian (TT) Division. The Essex Yeomanry were equipped with 25-pr Sextons, and had been trained for the assault for many months. The regiment was earmarked to provide close support for 8 Independent Armoured Brigade who was under command 50th Division for the landing.

Prior to the invasion all those taking part were locked up for security reasons in various camps. The regiment was in the New Forest. The guns were loaded onto Landing Craft Tanks (LCTs) at a hard near Beaulieu and we then collected with a lot of other LCTs alongside the Trans-Atlantic Ocean Terminal at Southampton on 3rd June. After setting sail on 4th June the fleet was halted for twenty-four hours off Yarmouth, Isle of Wight, in worsening weather.

There was one troop of four guns on each LCT. A sledge full of ammunition lay under each SP, to be towed ashore to augment the first line stocks, bringing the total amount of ammunition carried to over 300 rounds per gun. In addition some 200 rounds per gun were stacked for use in the preliminary bombardment, called the run-in shoot, which was fired from the LCTs prior to H-Hour.

Only tracked vehicles were taken on the assault. The rest of the space on the LCT was taken up with the OP tank and the Command Post tank (both Shermans) two half-tracks, and three carriers.

The fleet set sail on the evening of 5th June, in a long double column with massive air cover and an escort of destroyers.

Dawn on 6th June was clear but still windy. The regiment was reduced to five troops, the sixth having been unable to join the run-in shoot because its LCT had engine trouble during the night.

The tasks of 231 Brigade were to protect the right flank of 2nd Army until firm contact could be made with the American troops landing on Omaha beach ten miles away to the west; to capture Arromanches, which was to be the site of the British Mulberry Harbour, and Bessin, which was to be the terminal of the PLUTO fuel pipe-line. (This last operation included silencing the massive Longue Battery which menaced the whole area of the NEPTUNE/OVERLORD fleet.) 47th Marine Commando, who were under command of the brigade, were given the task of capturing Port-en-Bessin. 69 Brigade was to pass through and capture Bayeux, and 8 Armoured Brigade was to exploit to the south after supporting the Infantry onto their initial objectives.

The tasks of the close support artillery can best be illustrated by following the fortunes of 431 Battery of the Essex Yeomanry. C Troop got ashore and went into action on the beach at about H+20 and D Troop followed at H+40. The tide was almost up to the sea-wall but by driving the LCT in at half ahead together D Troop's LCT beached firmly and the troop got ashore without losing any of its vehicles. The troop was meant to go about 2 miles inland but, as the other two batteries were held up and it had been landed about a mile to the east of where it should have landed, the troop linked up with C Troop who were in action nearby on the beach.

The guns started firing immediately in support of the 1st Hampshires who were having difficulty clearing Le Hamel, which was their first objective. Additional ammunition was obtained from the LCT which had not taken part in the run-in shoot but which had been beached and become stranded nearby.

During the afternoon the battery moved inland and went into action near the Buhot cross-roads to join up with the other two batteries, which had succeeded in getting forward behind the 1st Dorsets. In the process one of their SPs had been used to knock out, at point-blank range, a very active large block-house that had been causing a lot of trouble along the beach and had destroyed three or four tanks of the Sherwood Rangers Yeomanry.

The regiment gave fire support for the assault on Arromanches, which fell in the evening without much of a struggle.

On D+1, 431 Battery was detached to support the Commandos' advance to Port-en-Bessin and went into action near La Riviere. We had been warned that we might have to meet a counter-attack from 2 SS Panzer Division. The rest of the regiment was supporting the advance on Bayeux, which was captured that day. 47th Commando had had a difficult time getting ashore. Although they got into Port-en-Bessin they were not strong enough to hold it. The Forward Observation Officer with them, who was the troop leader from C Troop deputising for his Troop Commander, was cut off but managed to escape during the night and get back to the battery position. During the day the 2nd Devons from 231 Brigade advanced along the coast and with fire support from the battery and the Royal Navy captured the Longue Battery, made contact with the Commandos and re-established the position in Port-en-Bessin. This was to be the junction point with the Americans but they were badly delayed on Omaha beach, so we had to hold it without them.

During the night of 8th June and under cover of a dawn mist, the Armoured Brigade with the Essex Yeomanry managed to slip through a gap in the German defences and establish themselves on point 103 overlooking Tilly-sur-Seules. 1st Dorsets also managed to get through to give support to the brigade. The guns went into action just behind the crest of the feature, which was established as a firm base by the armoured regiments of the brigade. The battery was on the left of the regimental position which was fairly tight. German infantry were on the ground when the guns arrived, but they withdrew to a farm about three hundred yards away and gave us no trouble.

During 9th June some Mark 4 tanks, of what we took to be part of 2 SS Panzer Division, were seen across the valley advancing down the main road to Bayeux and were slowed down by regimental concentrations. After heavy fighting the 1st Dorsets succeeded in getting into St Pierre.

On 10th June a heavy counter-attack drove the Dorsets back and the enemy recaptured part of St Pierre but his further advance was halted by 24th Lancers and 8 DLI (Who had joined us during the night.) The gun position came under heavy mortar and machine-gun fire as the main thrust of General von Bayerlein's Panzer Lehr Division was thrown against us.

On 11th June the regiment gave fire support to cover strong patrols by 4/7th RDG and the Sherwood Rangers Yeomanry and during the afternoon supported attacks by the Green Howards on the village of Cristot. While this was taking place the enemy launched a strong counter-attack from the area of Fontenay-le-Pesnel, which included air-burst shelling and heavy machine gun covering fire.

On 12th June the armoured regiments advanced to the Tilly-Fontenay road. Enemy AFVs and 88mm SPs were continuously engaged by the FOOs with the leading squadrons, but during the morning it became apparent that the enemy had made Tilly and Fontenay strong anti-tank localities which could not be forced by armour alone. An infantry brigade took over point 103 and as dusk fell the regiment withdrew to a position near Conde-sur-Seulles in support of 50th Division. For a Territorial Regiment which had not been in action before, much incident had been crowded into the first six days of battle. At times there were as many as ten FOOs with the armoured regiments and the supporting infantry. Although there were two troop leaders in D Troop, both were deployed continuously as FOOs. 431 Battery in fact fielded five FOOs on the beaches in the first hour of the assault on D-Day, one of them wading ashore at H-Hour with the first wave.

The extra experience that training can never produce was rapidly acquired, particularly the art of digging in quickly in order to survive the shelling and mortaring.

Confidence was established in radio. In the close battle on point 103 a regimental net was operated (an innovation at that time) which ensured a very rapid response to calls for fire support. Because the guns were so far forward the arc of fire was more than 180 degrees, well outside the traverse of the guns, with the result that the Tannoys (the loud-speaker communications between the command post and the guns) failed to work, as the cable got caught in the tracks, and we had to resort to the use of a megaphone. Because all the targets were fired at charge one we soon had a large pile of charge bags by each gun. Enemy mortar fire occasionally set these alight, which was an embarrassment when it happened at night. All of the battery commanders had been wounded by D+3 but the battery captains commanded the batteries with distinction until the BCs returned.

The Sextons provided excellent protection and there were very few casualties on the gun position.

By the end of the first week we had solved most of the teething problems and from then on we never looked back.

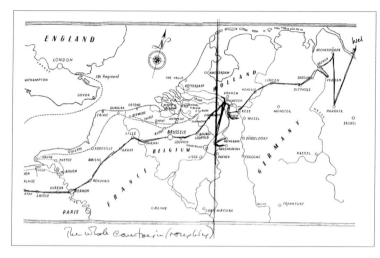

Campaign map (West). Courtesy of General Richardson.

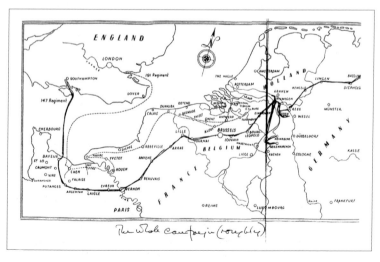

Campaign map (East). Courtesy of General Richardson.

MARKET GARDEN, SEPTEMBER 1944

[Taken from the article by Major General T.A. Richardson CB MBE in the *Journal of the Royal Artillery*]

Market Garden started with a massive fireplan on Sunday 17th September 1944, covering the attack by Guards Armoured Division down the road to Arnhem. 43rd Division with 8th Independent Armoured Brigade under command were tasked to follow through over the Arnhem Bridge directed on Zwolle and the Zuider Zee, with the task of securing all the bridges over the Ijssel river near the Dutch border with Germany.

In spite of the fireplan the 2nd (Armoured) Battalion Irish Guards lost their first nine Sherman tanks in quick succession as they advanced down the road to Eindhoven. At the same time 101 (US) Airborne Division landed near Veghel and Son. 82 (US) Airborne Division landed near Nijmegen in the area of Groesbeek and the first half of 1 (BR) Airborne Division landed near Arnhem. Unfortunately the main road bridge over the Wilhelmina Canal at Son was blown in the 101 Division area. On Monday 18th September 2nd Household Cavalry linked up with 101 Division, and the Irish Guards captured Eindhoven.

By 0600 hours on Tuesday 19th September 1944 the bridge at Son had been repaired and by 0800 hours the Household Cavalry had linked up with the 82 (US) AB Div at Grave. By 1200 hours the Armoured Regiment and Motor Battalion of the Grenadier Guards had crossed the bridge at Grave and that afternoon were in the outskirts of Nijmegen. A quickly mounted attack supported by the 25 pounder guns of the Leicestershire Yeomanry, who were part of the Guards Armoured Division, failed to capture the massive road and railway bridges over the Waal, which was strongly defended by elements of 10 Panzer Division.

In order to reinforce 82nd (US) AB Div and to enable them to hold the right flank, which was on the German Frontier near Nijmegen against an armoured threat, the Sherwood Rangers Yeomanry (SRY), from 8th Armoured Brigade, together with a company of the 12/60th and **413 Battery of the Essex Yeomanry** were pushed forward down the centre line on Tuesday evening, 19th September. Besides an overfull first line of ammunition the battery was accompanied by 12 RASC 3-tonners loaded with ammunition. After a 70 mile drive through the night they joined forces with 82 Div. At dawn. The squadron deployed in Mook, Wyler-Groesbeek and in the area of Beek and Bergen Daal, with the battery in action in the Dekkerswald among the crashed American gliders. This battery became the first British Artillery to fire into Germany. Without this reinforcement 82 Div would have been hard pressed to hold this open flank.

At 1500 hours on Wednesday 20th September 260 US Airborne soldiiers of 82 Div were ferried across the Waal by XXX Corps sappers. Simultaneously the Grenadier Guards attacked through Nijmegen. This combined assault resulted in the capture of both bridges over the Waal by last light. At that time there were no Germans except two light patrols defending Elst. The road to the Arnhem Bridge was wide open.

The same evening 8 Armoured Brigade and 214 Infantry Brigade of 43 Division were released down the centre line. Regimental HQ and the two remaining batteries of the **Essex Yeomanry (431 and 511)** were well forward in the order of march. Each SP was loaded with 300 rounds a gun and each battery was accompanied by 9 RASC 3-tonner loads of ammunition from 1680 RASC Ammunition Platoon (The Windmill Boys) who supplied us with ammunition and never failed us. It was a difficult night but, in spite of a total traffic jam at about 0200 hours, the guns were through to Nijmegen early on Thursday 21st September, and went into action near Hatert.

The same morning the Irish Guards Armoured Regiment and Infantry Battalion crossed the Waal bridge and attempted to break out of the bridgehead through Elst supported by the guns of the Leicestershire Yeomanry, which had also crossed into the bridgehead in order to cover the Irish Guards assault. By 0600 hours that morning the Germans had managed to move into Elst and establish a defensive line with 25 tanks and SPs and five battalions commanded by 10 SS Panzer Division. The Irish Guards were halted on the outskirts of Elstand and could not get through or round the small town.

That afternoon a further attack was planned. A column made up of 4/7 RDG (8 Brigade), 7 Somerset LI (214 Brigade) and **SP 431 Battery (Essex Yeomanry)** was asked to force its way through Elst to Arnhem Bridge at all costs. The leading Company of 7 SLI were to be mounted in Kangaroos (turretless Sherman tanks which were used as APCs). We were told that the road ran along a raised Bund. The guns were to be well forward in the column with only one infantry company and a half squadron of tanks in front of them. In order to br ready for any eventuality the guns were loaded with HE 119 cap on with the guns out of the clamps and alternately traversing fully left and right. Both the Somersets and **431 Battery** were ready to go with an hour or two of daylight to spare, but unfortunately the Germans managed to blow the main road bridge over the Maas-Waal canal at Weurt and the 4/7 RDG were delayed until after dark. It was deemed that the operation was impossible that night.

We were unaware that the Germans had captured Arnhem Bridge early that morning and with 10 SS Division defending Elst, we might have had a tough time trying to get through to Arnhem, but the diversion caused by the Polish AB Brigade landing at Driel that evening would have helped.

The Guns went back into action for the night and continued to harass the Germans in Elst and Oosterhout.

At dawn on Friday 22nd September the Household Cavalry managed to get round Elst and link up with the Polish AB Brigade which had dropped near Driel the previous evening. At 0700 hours that morning the guns of **431 and 511 Batteries Essex Yeomanry** crossed the Waal road bridge and went into action in Lent. 4/7 RDG and 7 SLI crossed the railway bridge and attacked the Germans in Oosterhout followed by the rest of 214 Brigade (5 DCLI and 1 Worcs). By the evening, after some fierce fighting, this force had reached Valburg. They pressed on during the night intermingled with retreating German tanks and linked up with the Poles at Driel. During this day the guns of the Leicestershire Yeomanry were withdrawn back across the Waal and as 43 Div guns were in action south of the river, the only field artillery in range of the hard pressed 1AB Div were the two batteries of the **Essex Yeomanry.**

On 23rd September 130 Brigade joined 214 Brigade, and the two batteries of **147 (Essex Yeomanry)** were moved forward to gun positions near Slijk-Ewijk, 112 (West Somerset Yeomanry) Field Regiment RA, part of 43 Div

Artillery, crossed the river and came into action near Oosterhaut. That night
we gave fire support to cover the Polish Brigade's attempt to cross the Neder
Rijn and join the rest of 1 AB Div.

On 24th September **511 Battery** moved forward to Gekvoort and **431** to
Valburg, west of Elst. 112 (West Somerset Yeomanry) also moved forward. By
this time 7 Medium Regiment were in action west of Nijmegen and were
giving fire support to both the west and the northeast. In the early hours
of 25th September a further extensive fireplan covered the crossing of the
Neder Rijn by 4 Dorset into 1 AB Div bridgehead. 43 Div launched a major
attack on Elst, which by this time was strongly held by the Germans with a
battle group reinforced by no less than 30 Tiger tanks.

On 25th September **431 Battery** moved again to Lijnden, midway
between Valburg and Elst. From this position we fired a considerable fireplan
to cover the withdrawal of 1 AB Div during a rather wet and dismal night.
SS Captain Moeller reported: *After nightfall the artillery bombardment intensified;
reports and impacts followed almost without let-up. The earth was trembling and
a curtain of fire and dirt of hitherto unknown dimensions rose over and between
our positions … and so it went on throughout the night without let-up.* The
Germans were unaware that 1 AB Div had withdrawn and thought more
reinforcements were coming across.

It was also in this gun position that we had a call for an SOS target in
the middle of the night to stave off a German counter-attack on Elst which
involved a switch of 179 degrees 30 minutes. Fortunately all the fire orders
had been given before the Tannoy box disappeared out of the Command
Post with the wires hooked around the tracks of the SPs as they tracked
round. No wonder we asked for all-round traverse for the next generation
of SP artillery after the war.

Between the 22nd and 26th September the centre line had been cut
behind us and a Brigade from the Guards Armoured Division was withdrawn
to deal with this threat. There were some advantages from this event. Brand
new ammunition was being flown into Grave and London Newspapers were
on occasions received the same day. The disadvantage was the fact that rations
were drawn from a German Army Depot and the German Army rations
were not up to British Army standards, especially as there was no tea, and
ersatz coffee made from acorns was issued instead.

On 23rd September the 43rd Reconnaissance Regiment and 12/60th
KRRC supported by **511 Battery Essex Yeomanry** had cleared the Island
down to its narrowest point to the west. This small force was reinforced on

27th September by a Brigade Group from 43 Div. **431 Battery** moved to Gekvoort to join with **511 Battery** in covering the west end of the Island and banks of the Neder Rijn to the north. During the next few days the Germans continued to reinforce the western end by means of a railway bridge over the Neder Rijn, which was still intact until destroyed by a very accurate Typhoon attack by the RAF. The bridge was clearly visible from the **Essex Yeomanry** OP near Ophheusden and it was just in range of the guns using supercharge. A bomb landed on one of the main supports of the bridge and tipped the whole of the centre section of the bridge into the river. It has never been rebuilt.

43 Div and 8th Armoured Brigade held these positions on the Island in spite of strong German counter attacks to regain Elst from the east and to sweep us off the Island from the west. The Island was eventually handed over to 101st US Airborne Division at the beginning of October. **431 and 511 Batteries** handed over their positions and withdrew from the Island on 3rd October and rejoined **413 Battery Essex Yeomanry**, who with the Sherwood Rangers Yeomanry and elements of the 32nd (US) Airborne Division had been holding the German border area to the east of Nijmegen. On 7th October the RAF tumbled the Arnhem Bridge into the Neder Rijn.

The failure of XXX Corps to link up with 1st Airborne Division has been discussed and debated in considerable detail. Perhaps if 506 Regiment of 101st (US) Airborne Division had managed to prevent the bridge at Son over the Wilhelmina Canal north of Eindhoven being blown, which delayed XXX Corps for 24 hours, the story might have been very different.

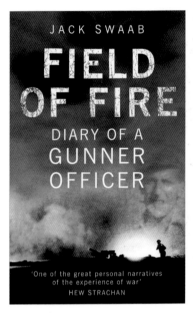

JACK SWAAB

FIELD OF FIRE

DIARY OF A GUNNER OFFICER

'One of the great personal narratives
of the experience of war'
HEW STRACHAN

Field of Fire
Jack Swaab

Jack Swaab joined the 51st (Highland)
Infantry Division in 1943. His diaries
record two and a half years of service,
and the alternating boredom and fear
that characterises wartime soldiering.
  In 1943 he fought with Montgomery
at the Mareth Line, and took part in
the Allied landings on Sicily. In 1944 his
regiment prepared for D-Day, and he
became a forward observation officer,
working closely alongside the infantry.
  He was again selected for FOO duty
during the Rhine crossing, and was
wounded by shellfire, earning the
Military Cross.

978 0 7509 4276 8

£8.99

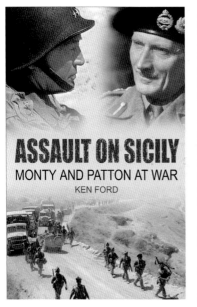

Assault on Sicily
Ken Ford

In July 1943, the Allies launched
an armada of 2,590 vessels against
Sicily, in one of the largest combined
operations of the war.

It was the only action where the
whole Allied war effort was brought
to bear on a single objective, with one
army commanded by Montgomery
and one commanded by Patton. Both
men were insubordinate egotists,
always choosing to do their own
thing, regardless of others' sensibilities.

It was in Sicily that the seeds of their
rivalry were sown, which were reaped
in the campaigns following D-Day.

978 0 7509 4301 7

£19.99

Hilke's Diary
edited by Geseke Clark

Hilke's Diary is a battered chintz-covered little book with a flowery pattern, its lock long-since broken. It was the inseparable companion of a little girl growing up in Germany during the Second World War.

It talks of her evacuation – the pain of homesickness and the challenge of life with a strange family, and then at boarding school - turning into a story of survival and triumph. It is also an account of a young teenager who yearns to be a patriot, but whose heart cannot be reconciled with the suffering brought about by the war.

978 0 7524 4513 7

£8.99

If you are interested in purchasing other books published by Tempus,
or in case you have difficulty finding any Tempus books in your local bookshop,
you can also place orders directly through our website

www.thehistorypress.co.uk